## Praise for
### *Reaching the World in Our*

"In most communities here in America, you will find yourself in a global village. If you want to be sensitized as to the urgency of witnessing cross-culturally to expatriates, and if you want to be tutored on how to do it effectively, this book will be of great help to you."

> —TONY CAMPOLO, PH.D., Eastern University

"An absolute wealth of insightful information for sharing Christ with those of different cultures who cross our paths daily. An exceedingly helpful book, which I cannot recommend highly enough."

> —M. BLAINE SMITH, director of Nehemiah Ministries
> and author of *Knowing God's Will*

"Everyone who is serious about personal evangelism should have a copy of this book. Rajendra Pillai has provided an encyclopedia of information on people of other cultures, making it accessible and breaking down barriers with his breezy, easy-to-read format. It's hard to believe this wealth of information could be available in such a manageable package."

> —CAROLYN CURTIS, author and editor of *On Mission*

"*Reaching the World in Our Own Backyard*…is a practical manual for sharing Christ with the most culturally diverse nation on earth. Rajendra tackles a tough topic—evangelism—without losing his whimsical but powerful style."

> —MICHAEL R. SMITH, PH.D., School of Communication and the Arts,
> Department of Journalism, Regent University

"Ready or not, we are all cross-cultural missionaries right where we live. If we are serious about helping people of other cultures and religions understand the gospel message, we need this book. Rajendra Pillai has given us an excellent tool."

> —DR. ROGER C. PALMS, author of fifteen books
> and former editor of Billy Graham's *Decision* magazine

"A great handbook for today's Christians in witnessing to people of other cultures, religions, and worldviews. It brings a strong message in dealing with wrong attitudes and responses to those of other cultures and serves as a guide in understanding people of diverse cultural backgrounds."

—MARILYN LASZLO, author of *Mission Possible* and linguist-translator with Wycliffe Bible Translators

"Finally! A practical guide for the ordinary Christian. As the apostle Paul's Epistles equip the saints to live the Christian life, *Reaching the World in Our Own Backyard* equips today's believers to carry out the Great Commission. In a very straightforward and compassionate way, Rajendra Pillai kindles the desire within us and encourages us to reach out to people of other cultures and faiths in this country."

—SHARON L. DYSON, PH.D., consultant and trainer

"*Reaching the World in Our Own Backyard* moves beyond theory into the realm of practical application. From the initial approach to dealing with rejection to leading a person of another culture to the Savior, this book lays a solid foundation and offers practical guidelines for those of us who truly desire to reach the world—the one that exists in our neighborhoods, schools, and places of employment—for Christ!"

—DAVID GOUGH, chairman of the Department of Educational Ministries, Washington Bible College, Lanham, Maryland

"How exciting to finally have a reference that is thoroughly written, yet concise and easily understood, designed specifically to assist in interpersonal information and understanding with cultural and religious differences in mind! Anyone wishing to understand and reach out to those from cultures other than their own can use this book in work, travel, and the day-to-day life of this increasingly globalized planet Earth."

—BETTIE ANN BRIGHAM, dean of Eastern University, St. Davids, Pennsylvania

# reaching the world in
# our own
# backyard

# reaching the world in
# our own
# backyard

a guide to building relationships with people of other faiths and cultures

## RAJENDRA K. PILLAI

WATERBROOK
PRESS

REACHING THE WORLD IN OUR OWN BACKYARD
PUBLISHED BY WATERBROOK PRESS
2375 Telstar Drive, Suite 160
Colorado Springs, Colorado 80920
*A division of Random House, Inc.*

Details in some anecdotes and stories have been changed to protect the identities of the persons involved.

ISBN 1-57856-601-0

Library of Congress Cataloging-in-Publication Data

Pillai, Rajendra.
  Reaching the world in our own backyard : a guide to building relationships with people of other faiths and cultures / Rajendra Pillai.—1st ed.
    p. cm.
  Includes bibliographical references.
  ISBN 1-57856-601-0
  1. Intercultural communication—Religious aspects—Christianity. 2. Intercultural communi-cation—United States. 3. Evangelistic work—United States. 4. Witness bearing (Christianity) I. Title.
BV2082 .I57P55 2003
248'.5—dc21                                                                                    2003001154

Printed in the United States of America
2003—First Edition

10 9 8 7 6 5 4 3 2 1

*I dedicate this book to the woman*
*whose smile rekindles my heart and whose presence warms my soul—*
*my wife and best friend, Erika.*
*Without her love, vision, and constant encouragement,*
*this book would not have been possible.*

# Contents

## PART 3: HOW TO PRESENT THE GOSPEL TO PEOPLE OF OTHER RELIGIONS

# Foreword

Not that many years ago, I would have seen little purpose for a book titled *Reaching the World in Our Own Backyard.*

Times have definitely changed. The moment for this message has arrived.

America is a different land from the one I grew up in during the previous century. Back home on our farm in Indiana, there was no "world in our backyard." Sure, we recognized that the United States was a "melting pot" of people from many lands and cultures, but most of them lived in large cities far away. The most diversity we enjoyed was driving an hour to the nearest Kmart or playing with the Amish children who lived on surrounding farms. But by and large, the people we knew were mainly folks just like us.

At that time most of our exposure to the broader world came through the media. Of course, the sophisticates among us enjoyed "foreign" foods such as French fries, Swedish meatballs, Mexican tacos, and German sauerkraut! At high school we might have befriended an occasional exchange student. But our most meaningful contact with the world came when international missionaries spoke at church and visited our home. We juvenile Haggards gazed wide-eyed at their pictures and were amazed at their stories of foreign adventure. But they quickly went back to their distant fields while we went back to feeding the livestock, plowing the fields, and playing baseball.

That insulated existence no longer exists for the vast majority of Americans. The old saying that "we are all missionaries" is truer than ever. Now, even if we live in America's heartland, far away from the exotic coasts or major cities, we often encounter visitors and fellow citizens from the ends of the earth. In virtually every neighborhood and community, "the world" now lives next door, owns the restaurant at the mall, staffs the doctor's office down the street, or studies at the school desk across the aisle. The taxi drivers and hotel workers we meet are often people who love freedom and opportunity, those who have left familiar surroundings to test their skills in a nation that gives them an opportunity to serve others with the potential of great reward.

This gives us an unprecedented opening to spread the gospel on a daily basis to people of "every tongue and nation"—without having to go anywhere.

Rajendra Pillai's book *Reaching the World in Our Own Backyard* is the book our generation can use to build strong friendships with people from other countries and, during that process, to gain a hearing for why we believe in Jesus Christ.

Increasingly, missiologists say that one of the more effective and efficient ways to get the gospel to the most secluded places in the world is to reach those who are visiting our nation to get an education. All of us who live near a university or a training center can help complete the Great Commission by simply becoming a host family to foreign students. Touch them with the love of Christ, and when they go home to a position of influence within their own communities, the warmth of Christ will go with them.

No doubt God placed the vision for the message of this book in Rajendra's heart while he was young. Born in India, Rajendra learned how to interact on a daily basis with the Hindus and Muslims in his Calcutta neighborhood. As a Christian he experienced firsthand what it feels like to be a religious minority. Now living in America, Rajendra's sensitivity to the needs of individuals from other lands and cultures shows through on every page.

Here is a sampling of the interesting and often surprising demographic facts on our changing country that you will discover in *Reaching the World in Our Own Backyard*:

- In many big cities and counties of the United States, it is not unusual to find residents from more than one hundred countries conversant in more than one hundred languages.
- Between 1990 and 2000, the number of foreign-born residents in the United States increased by 50 percent.
- More than one-half million foreign students are studying at U.S. colleges and universities.
- Islam is the fastest growing religion both in the world and in the United States. For example, in the Chicago area there are more Muslims than Methodists and more Buddhists than Episcopalians.
- In 2002 about sixty million internationals paid a visit to the United States.

- One in five of America's schoolchildren speaks a language other than English at home.
- The majority (50 percent) of Arab Americans are Christian. Only 23 percent are Muslim.

More important, however, *Reaching the World in Our Own Backyard* is not just statistics and analysis. It is a passionate cry for American Christians to join the cause of world evangelization by learning how to communicate with and love people from across the globe who now live in their ZIP code. An entire section of the book, a type of encyclopedia on how to relate interculturally, offers basic behavioral tips and simple language phrases to enhance communication with individuals from fifty-two nations—Algeria to Zimbabwe.

In other informative passages you will learn—

- The seven signs of *ineffective* cross-cultural evangelism and the three elements of *effective* cross-cultural evangelism.
- The differences between "low-context" cultures like our own and "high-context" cultures found predominantly in Asia, Africa, and Latin America. (A person from a low-context culture depends primarily on words to communicate, whereas a person from a high-context culture is more influenced by gestures, eye contact, and body language.)
- Guidelines on relating to new arrivals to America—good, practical advice such as, "Above all, practice the universal code for instilling reassurance in a fellow human being: Smile!"

In another section Rajendra provides a concise but helpful overview of how to interact with and present the gospel to followers of all major world religions.

If you learn what this book teaches, the next time you encounter a person from a foreign land, you will have the basic tools to initiate a productive relationship. This could mean the difference between life and death for someone; the stakes are that high as we assist in advancing God's kingdom on earth.

Rajendra quotes a friend who wisely says, "People come to Christ best on the arm of a friend."

This book will help you become that friend to someone who needs the best news ever shared.

—TED HAGGARD

# Acknowledgments

For two years as I worked on this manuscript, many people lent me their support, both in practical advice and prayer. I am grateful to my church, Damascus Road Community Church in Damascus, Maryland, and its members for their encouragement and prayer throughout the process of getting this book ready. I am proud to be part of such a loving, caring, and joyful congregation. I am also thankful to my senior pastor, Dr. Richard Fredericks, and his wife, Sallie, for their prayers and inspiration as I worked on this book.

Many of my wonderful friends enthusiastically looked over sections dealing with their specific countries or former religions and gave additional valuable insights. I am grateful to Manish and Janice Chanda, Michael Braga, Paul and Jen Propson, David Kuguru, Tom Ogunde, Edwin Calanog, Michael Ortiz, Gary Goldberg, Hamish Crooks, Pascal Foucault, Swinitha Osuri, Tony Pereira, Armando Osorio, Ena Bromley, and Mabelle Manjivar.

Many thanks to my writers' group in Maryland—Alexander Clayborne, Ron Knoll, Susan Hamilton, Sheree Parris Nudd, and Christine Thron—for their suggestions and comments. I am also grateful to two of my closest buddies, Michael Braga in England and Joseph Appaswamy in India, for their friendship. They believed and encouraged me to believe that I did have this book inside of me!

Special thanks also to my dear friends Solomon and Lori Wang and Joyce Druart—all three of whom are champions for Jesus—for their encouragement.

I want to offer my heartfelt appreciation to the most beautiful woman I have ever set my eyes on—my wife and best friend, Erika—for her enthusiasm and the hours she spent reading this manuscript and for her valuable insights. A note of gratitude as well to my other mother, my mother-in-law, Suellen Velthuis, for her encouragement and suggestions.

Finally, I want to thank my agent, Joyce Hart, and my editors at WaterBrook Press, Erin Healy and Dan Benson, as well as Laura Barker and Jennifer Lonas, for their vision, encouragement, and constant support, which made this book a reality.

# How to Use This Book

A book of this nature obviously depends on scores of different sources. In preparation for writing the sections on various countries and religions, I consulted embassies, travel brochures, dozens of books, numerous magazine articles, encyclopedias, and people from those specific countries and religious backgrounds in order to present the most accurate information possible. However, I am aware that other pertinent details may exist that could make this material even more effective. If you know of any, please send them to me at the address listed at the end of this introduction.

If you feel something stated in this book is not entirely accurate, please understand that the guidelines presented on different countries and religions are *general* pointers that apply in most cases. As you interact with people of other cultures and religions, you will find that those with varied life experiences approach customs and traditions differently. For this reason, I have provided the most commonly known norms. I would love, however, to hear about your own experiences.

Throughout this book I refer to recent immigrants, foreign students, and tourists as *internationals*. Whenever you come across this term, keep in mind that it includes people who have only recently arrived in the United States. By *recent*, I mean within the last thirty years or so.

I also want to mention here that the statistics in this book have been taken from *The World Almanac and Book of Facts, 2002.* Languages and phrases have been collected from hundreds of sources. If there are other common forms of greetings or if a better alternative to something mentioned in this book is available, I would be delighted to include them in future editions of this book. Also, in many countries the same word can be pronounced in a variety of ways in different parts of the country. I have included the pronunciation that, according to my research, is most widely used. For languages that use a non-Roman script—such as Chinese or Japanese—I have written the greetings as they would be pronounced. Translations of some phrases are not always literal—sometimes the closest equivalent of a greeting is all that can be provided. Keep in mind that your international friend may pronounce the same word differently. The idea is to build a bridge; just a sincere attempt on your part to speak the language will help create rapport and will mean a lot to your international friend.

*Reaching the World in Our Own Backyard* is not intended as a theological debate on different religions or as a thesis on diverse cultures of the world. It is not a book on pluralistic issues, affirmative action, equal opportunity, or immigration policies, nor is it an exhaustive description or comparison of world cultures and religions. Rather, it is intended as a general reference guide for the busy Christian—a quick snapshot of various cultures and religions.

My aim in this book is to encourage and motivate, equip and inspire Christians in this nation to share Jesus Christ with their international friends. My desire is that we would reach out and learn to relate to people whose ethnicity, culture, and religion is different from ours and that we would do this by being culturally sensitive and doctrinally pure. We can achieve this goal by knowing at least a little about the cultures and religions of those with whom we are attempting to develop relationships.

Hopefully, this book will help you understand more fully that Christians have a vast new mission field in America that, until now, has been largely overlooked. Most of us find it difficult to relate to people of other cultures; we like being in our own groups. Yet the Lord has provided a ready harvest field right in our own backyard.

As you begin, prayerfully read part 1, which provides helpful information on recent demographic changes, typical ways Americans react to internationals, and how best to become equipped to reach people of other cultures and religions.

Then look up specific pointers under the country and religion sections to learn how to relate to a person from a certain background. The information in this book provides important, basic details. It is meant as a quick read—information you can review and apply right away.

For those who are interested in learning about other cultures and religions in greater detail, a list of recommended resources is provided at the end of various sections throughout the book and in the bibliography.

If the Lord births a desire in your heart to reach the internationals in your community, you might consider starting a ministry in your church. Suggestions are offered in the epilogue.

My prayer is that our Lord may use *Reaching the World in Our Own Back-yard* to inspire and equip you to reach people of other cultures and religions in this great nation. Please feel free to write to me about your experiences.

—RAJENDRA PILLAI
P.O. Box 255
Clarksburg, MD 20871-0255

Part 1

# America's Greatest Opportunity

# 1

# What's Your Cultural Quotient?

One of the most surprising things internationals experience in the United States is the apparent absence of world news. American newspapers, television, and radio networks operate primarily in a concentric circle—local news, state news, and national news, with very little space or time given to world news.

This is surprising to internationals, because in most countries, people take pride in keeping abreast of world events or current affairs. In American society many media outlets promote themselves as the source "where local news comes first." This has led to a degree of isolation from what is happening overseas and around the world.

In many big cities and counties of the United States, it is not unusual to find residents from more than one hundred countries conversant in more than one hundred languages. If we are to reach these people for whom Christ died, we need to make an effort to learn more about them and their homelands.

So here's the fun part. I have designed a fascinating quiz that will take you on a whirlwind tour of recent U.S. demographic changes and of various world cultures you may encounter in your daily life. You won't be graded on this, but hopefully you will find the information both interesting and eyeopening. After you've taken the quiz, check your answers against the key provided at the end of the chapter to see how well you did.

## TEST YOUR CULTURAL QUOTIENT

1. The number of foreign-born residents in the United States has increased by what percentage between 1990 and 2000?
   a. 10 percent
   b. 24 percent
   c. 32 percent
   d. 50 percent

2. According to a Council on American-Islamic Relations survey of mosques in the United States, what percentage of converts to Islam are white?
   a. 4 percent
   b. 13 percent
   c. 18 percent
   d. 27 percent

3. In the United States, what is the average percentage of converts or brand-new Muslims in each mosque?
   a. 5 percent
   b. 10 percent
   c. 15 percent
   d. 30 percent

4. What percentage of African American Muslims is connected to Louis Farrakhan's Nation of Islam?
   a. less than 3 percent
   b. 10 percent
   c. 25 percent
   d. more than 50 percent

5. According to the 2000 U.S. Census, what ratio of Americans are Hispanic, Black, Asian, or of two or more races?
   a. 1 in 4
   b. 1 in 8
   c. 1 in 10
   d. 1 in 17

6. In 1999 most immigrants to the United States came from Mexico. Which country ranked second?

   a. China

   b. Philippines

   c. India

   d. El Salvador

7. Most Arab Americans are:

   a. Muslims

   b. Christians

   c. Atheists

   d. members of orthodox religions

8. The fastest growing religion in the United States is

   a. Christianity

   b. Hinduism

   c. Buddhism

   d. Islam

9. The statement "Most Arab Americans were born in the United States" is:

   a. True

   b. False

10. What is the average number of Muslims associated with a mosque in the United States?

    a. less than 100

    b. 600

    c. 1,100

    d. more than 1,600

11. In 1999 how many international visitors (tourists, business people, etc.) visited the United States?

    a. less than 10 million

    b. 20 million

    c. 30 million

    d. nearly 50 million

12. How much did these tourists spend, and how many American jobs were supported by their spending?
    a. $11 billion/210,000 jobs
    b. $27 billion/330,000 jobs
    c. $53 billion/560,000 jobs
    d. $75 billion/1.1 million jobs

13. In 1999, 32.3 million people in the United States were classified as poor. Most of these people were
    a. Asians
    b. Whites
    c. Blacks
    d. Hispanics

14. What ratio of America's school-age children speak a language other than English at home?
    a. 1 in 5
    b. 1 in 10
    c. 1 in 20
    d. 1 in 50

15. The 2000 Census allowed respondents to select more than one race for the first time in U.S. history. How many people selected more than one race?
    a. 1.1 million
    b. 2.3 million
    c. 4.7 million
    d. 6.8 million

16. Between 1990 and 2000, the number of Asian Indians (who are mostly Hindus) in the United States grew to a record 1.6 million. This reflects a growth of
    a. 25 percent
    b. 50 percent
    c. 75 percent
    d. 100 percent

What's Your Cultural Quotient?    7

17. According to the 2000 Census, how many states now have a white minority?
    a.  0
    b.  1
    c.  2
    d.  3

18. More than one-half million foreign students are studying at U.S. colleges and universities. Which country sent the largest number of students in 2000?
    a.  China
    b.  India
    c.  Brazil
    d.  Canada

19. What percentage of people currently entering the American work force are women and minorities?
    a.  35 percent
    b.  45 percent
    c.  55 percent
    d.  85 percent

20. What should you never give as a gift to a Hindu?
    a.  a carving knife
    b.  a leather wallet
    c.  a folding umbrella
    d.  chocolate-chip cookies

21. What should you avoid serving to a Buddhist who comes to your house for a meal?
    a.  stir-fried carrots, broccoli, and water chestnuts
    b.  beef stroganoff
    c.  chicken casserole
    d.  egg-noodle soup

22. Between 1990 and 2000, the number of people who called themselves Christians in the United States

a. remained the same at 91 percent of the total population

b. decreased 9 percent from 86 percent to 77 percent of the total population

c. increased 10 percent from 80 percent to 90 percent of the total population

d. increased 1 percent from 85 percent to 86 percent of the total population

23. Suppose your new neighbors are from China, and you want to build a relationship with them. You decide to take a meal and a gift to them—but what gift must you avoid giving?

a. a fruit basket with apples, oranges, and bananas

b. a box of chocolates

c. a Mickey Mouse clock

d. a set of good quality pens

24. Brazilians don't like being called:

a. Hispanics

b. Brazilians

c. South Americans

d. Americans

25. A gentleman from Egypt has just arrived in the United States. He steps into your church out of curiosity, so you introduce yourself and start talking to him. Suddenly, you notice he is standing very close to you and leans right over your shoulder as he talks to you. What should you do?

a. Back off.

b. Stay where you are.

c. Tell him he is standing too close.

d. Lean over his shoulder when talking to him.

26. You meet an Indonesian family. They have a cute eight-year-old boy. What must you never do when greeting the child?

a. Say hello in English.

b. Shake hands with the child.

    c.  Pat the child's head.

    d.  Lightly touch the child's cheeks.

27. Suppose a foreign student named Muhammad has just arrived in the United States from Saudi Arabia with his wife and three kids. You get to know them, and they invite you over to their house. Which of the actions below could greatly offend your new Saudi friends?

    a.  offering to remove your shoes before you enter the house

    b.  talking about Saudi culture

    c.  showing a thumbs-up gesture when you agree with something

    d.  inviting them to your house for dinner

28. You are invited to the home of Chinese friends. You attempt to eat with chopsticks, which is greatly appreciated by your Chinese hosts. After the meal, what is the proper way to put the chopsticks away?

    a.  Place them on the table.

    b.  Place them parallel on top of the bowl.

    c.  Cross them and place them on top of the bowl.

    d.  Drop them to the floor.

29. When eating with an Asian Indian, you should avoid

    a.  talking

    b.  drinking water

    c.  using your left hand

    d.  using your fingers to place food in your mouth

## BUILDING BRIDGES

So how did you do? As you go through this book, you will learn more about the interesting customs and traditions of people of other cultures and religions. The fact is, as we move toward a more multicultural society, we need to be aware of what might offend or insult someone from another culture.

People from other cultures who live in the United States realize that Americans may not know their customs and traditions, and they are usually eager to talk with us about their ways of life. Many of these people don't know the Lord. As Christians, it is important for us to build bridges to those who feel alienated and misunderstood, for these are often the least-evangelized people groups in America. Jesus built bridges to the bypassed people groups of His time—tax collectors, lepers, prostitutes, Samaritans, poor people, and so on. Should we do any less?

## Answers to Quiz

1. d—50 percent. There were 20 million foreign-born residents in the United States in 1990. This number reached 30 million by the year 2000.
2. d—27 percent
3. d—30 percent. Based on a study by the Council on American-Islamic Relations of over 1,200 mosques in the United States.
4. a—less than 3 percent
5. a—1 in 4
6. b—Philippines
7. b—Christians. More than 50 percent are Christians. Only 23 percent are Muslims.
8. d—Islam
9. a—true
10. d—more than 1,600. Based on a study by the Council on American-Islamic Relations of over 1,200 mosques in the United States.
11. d—nearly 50 million
12. d—$75 billion/1.1 million jobs
13. b—Whites. Sixty-eight percent of all poor people were white.
14. a—1 in 5
15. d—6.8 million
16. d—100 percent
17. d—3: California, Hawaii, and New Mexico
18. a—China
19. d—85 percent

20.   b—a leather wallet. Hindus consider the cow to be a holy animal. They don't eat beef, and devout Hindus avoid using leather products, especially since most are made from cowhides.

21.   b—beef stroganoff. Buddhists don't eat beef. Keep in mind that some Buddhists are vegetarians so (c) and (d) will also apply in those cases.

22.   b—decreased 9 percent from 86 percent to 77 percent of the total population

23.   c—a Mickey Mouse clock. Clocks are associated with funerals.

24.   a—Hispanic. *Hispanic* literally means "Spanish speaking," and Brazilians speak Portuguese. They are linguistically and culturally different from people of all other Latin American countries.

25.   b—stay where you are. Egyptians have a much smaller "personal space" than Americans. Backing off is a mistake; your Egyptian friend will simply step forward to close the gap.

26.   c—pat the child's head. The head is considered sacred by Indonesians and should never be touched (not even to pat a child).

27.   c—showing a thumbs-up gesture when you agree with something. The thumbs-up gesture is considered very offensive in Saudi Arabia.

28.   a—place them on the table. All others are signs of bad luck and will offend your Chinese hosts.

29.   c—using your left hand. The left hand is considered unclean in India and in many other countries. Always use your right hand for eating as well as for receiving and giving things.

# 2

# America's Greatest Opportunity

You have new neighbors who just moved into a house next door. Their skin color is different from yours, they speak a different language, they eat different kinds of food, and their voices resonate with a thick foreign accent. You know they aren't Christians because they have portraits of their gods hanging on their walls. As a Christian you want to establish a friendship with them and tell them about your faith in Jesus Christ.

But how?

## The Demographics

According to the U.S. Census Bureau, more than thirty million people presently living in this country were born *outside* the United States. Approximately 44 percent of them arrived during the 1990s. Furthermore, the U.S. Department of Commerce estimates that more than fifty-six million visitors and tourists came into the United States in the year 2000, fueling a $100 billion tourism industry. The number of visitors was estimated at nearly sixty million in 2002. There are also about one-half million foreign students in the United States, many from countries that have traditionally resisted the gospel.

In the Chicago area there are more Muslims than Methodists and more Buddhists than Episcopalians. While the number of people from other religions has grown exponentially, the number of Christians has declined. The United Methodist Church has declined almost 24 percent since 1965. The number of Episcopalians has decreased by 36 percent.

In 2000 the Council on American-Islamic Relations conducted a survey of more than twelve hundred mosques in the United States. The survey revealed that 30 percent of Muslims in America associated with these mosques were converts. What percentage of Christians in an average church are converts? I don't have an exact figure, but I suspect it is far less than 30 percent. A full 27 percent of those Muslim converts were whites, breaking the stereotype that most Muslims in America are African Americans.

The number of people who call themselves Christian has decreased 9 percent since 1990, from 86 percent to 77 percent of the total population.* About sixty-five million people in America do not consider themselves Christian. Even among those who call themselves Christian, many are nominal in their beliefs, not having a full understanding of what it means to be truly saved.

Many churches are losing members. Those that are gaining members are increasing more through the migration of Christians from other churches than by making new converts. Perhaps it is not so stunning to hear Robert C. Neville, dean of the Boston University School of Theology, say in the *Boston Globe* that "Christendom has collapsed."

## Is There a Problem?

Many Christians don't want to acknowledge that there may be a problem. Many of us are happy with our snug, predictable suburban lives, where we fulfill our religious responsibilities by attending church once a week. Churches across the nation are hurting because only a miniscule percentage of their members want to get involved in any way other than showing up for the weekly service. This often leads to the problem of overworking those people who do volunteer. They in turn become burned out and then don't want to get involved again. So the vicious cycle continues.

A Christian lady once told me, "You have to be very careful about getting

---

* Pamela Paul, "One Nation Under God?" *American Demographics,* January 2002, 16-7.

involved in the church. Once you volunteer for something, you are stuck with it for life."

Is this the kind of devotion we have for the Lord's work? Pastors and church staff struggle constantly to operate ministries for which church members are not willing to volunteer. Sure, I believe strongly in leading a balanced lifestyle—but most, if not all, Christians can get involved in at least one ministry in their church. What a remarkable place the church would become if this were to happen!

Furthermore, many of us are so uncomfortable about sharing the gospel—especially with people of other cultures and religions—that we are content to live with the lie that evangelism is the job of the pastor and the church staff. Some of us are even embarrassed to talk with others about Jesus. Yet Jesus made it clear that if we are ashamed of Him and the gospel now, then He will be ashamed of us throughout eternity. (See Mark 8:38.) The Enemy has done well in deceiving us; let's not allow him any more ground.

We must view people from other cultures and religions as exactly what they are without Christ: eternally lost. Those of us who call ourselves Christians have a Christ-ordained mandate and obligation to take the gospel to them. However, for most of us, this is easier said than done.

*Reaching the World in Our Own Backyard* offers insights and information about each of the major non-Christian religions in America. To help you avoid embarrassing situations or making cultural gaffes that will offend others, you will learn the basic cultural norms of people from other countries. You will then be able to enjoy meaningful dialogue with someone of another religion or culture. In short, my ultimate goal throughout this book is to equip you to build friendships and eventually share your faith in Jesus Christ with your international friends.

## THE COMMUNITY THEY SEEK

Remember that many internationals—especially those from Asian, African, Latin American, and Eastern European countries—come from collectivist societies. This means that people from these countries consider being part of a *group* more important than do those from individualistic cultures such as North America or Western Europe.

One of the first things that strikes people from other cultures when they come to the United States is the lack of community to which they can connect. This is where the church can step in to fill a vital need. (If you want to learn more about starting a ministry to internationals in your church, read the epilogue.)

When Jesus said, "Go and make disciples of all nations" (Matthew 28:19), He wasn't speaking just to pastors and church leaders. He was speaking to each of us who calls Him Lord. Recent demographic changes have brought the world to our doorstep. We don't necessarily have to travel to distant lands to take the gospel to Asians, Latin Americans, Europeans, or Africans. They are right here in our own backyard, our neighborhood, and our community.

## SEVEN SIGNS OF INEFFECTIVE CROSS-CULTURAL EVANGELISM

As we begin preparing ourselves to be *effective* witnesses among people of other cultures, let's consider seven factors that make a person *ineffective* in cross-cultural evangelism:

1. *Making fun of someone else's beliefs or country of origin.* You may think that making fun of a person's country or beliefs will break the ice and loosen everyone up, but it may also backfire. For instance, a joke among the Japanese goes this way: "What do you call a person who knows two languages? Bilingual. What do you call a person who knows only one language? American." Now, the Japanese may find this funny, but do you? The reverse is also true: It is okay for people to make jokes about their own culture, but it is never okay for you and me to make jokes about it.

2. *Labeling belief in other gods and goddesses as "satanic."* This kind of simplistic and highly offensive attitude will totally turn off your listener. If a Buddhist came up to you and insisted that Jesus is an evil god, how likely is it that you would be receptive to anything he had to say about Buddha?

3. *Getting into an argument or a heated debate.* Will winning an argument convince the listener that the gospel is true? Not likely. The fact is, winning an argument rarely wins a soul. We should avoid "meaningless talk" (1 Timothy 1:6). Our job is to proclaim the gospel, not to win an argument.

4. *Witnessing only to people within your own group.* We should reach out to people outside our own group, working to break down our stereotypes and drop our biases. Christ died for *all* people.

5. *Insisting that internationals conform to American culture.* Many internationals have strong religious and cultural traditions and customs that they practice within the confines of their homes and places of worship. Arab Americans have a saying, "Truly Arab and fully American," which typifies how they seek to integrate their faith and culture with the American lifestyle. In order to be effective, we need to understand and respect people's beliefs and traditions. Once they know we care, they will want to know more about our faith and beliefs.

6. *Keeping the pressure on someone until he or she makes a decision to accept Christ.* We are called to be witnesses, but we cannot save anyone. Only God can. As my senior pastor, Dr. Richard Fredericks, puts it, "We are beggars telling other beggars where to find food." Again, our primary work is to share the gospel, but we must leave the results to God and be sensitive as to whether a person is ready to make a decision. Certainly, if we feel someone is ready to commit, we should offer our help. But to pester someone who isn't ready to make a decision is a sure way to cause that person to avoid you and the gospel in the future.

7. *Including lots of Christian terminology and jargon in your discussions.* Many Christian terms such as *convicted, conversion, sanctification,* and *justification* are meaningless and baffling to non-Christians. So when you share your testimony, try to give a clear explanation of how and why you became a Christian as well as a simple overview of the gospel.

## A Foundation for Effective Cross-Cultural Evangelism

It is God's desire to build His kingdom among people from all cultures. If we believe in the Bible, then we must also believe that our African friends, Asian coworkers, and Latino neighbors have all descended from Adam and Eve just as we have. As mentioned above, Christ made it very clear that we are to preach the gospel to *all* nations.

In contrast to the signs of ineffective evangelism outlined above, the following three elements form a foundation for *effective* cross-cultural evangelism:

1. *Catch God's heartbeat.* One of the best-known verses in the Bible quotes the final words of Jesus before He ascended to heaven: "But you will receive power when the Holy Spirit comes on you; and you will be my witnesses in

Jerusalem, and in all Judea and Samaria, and to the ends of the earth" (Acts 1:8). Notice the ever-widening circle: It starts in Jerusalem (our communities), expands to Judea and Samaria (our nation), and proceeds to the ends of the earth (the world).

*Our God is a multicultural God.* He desires that people from every part of the earth worship Him. He has called us to build a community of believers consisting of people from all over the world. Imagine what would happen if Christians in every American locality took the gospel to their neighbors and communities! What a profound impact we could have upon society if we took this principle to heart!

2. *Enter into people's worlds.* In the gospel of John, we read an amazing story of cross-cultural love in action:

> [Jesus] left Judea and went back once more to Galilee. Now he had to go through Samaria. So he came to a town in Samaria called Sychar.... Jacob's well was there, and Jesus, tired as he was from the journey, sat down by the well. It was about the sixth hour. When a Samaritan woman came to draw water, Jesus said to her, "Will you give me a drink?"... The Samaritan woman said to him, "You are a Jew and I am a Samaritan woman. How can you ask me for a drink?" (John 4:3-9)

Samaritans were of a mixed race, and Jews were known to hate Samaritans. Jews deliberately avoided going through Samaria and resisted any contact with Samaritans. By talking to the Samaritan woman, Jesus broke one of the huge cross-cultural mores of His day. In fact, He took another shot at Jewish-Samaritan hatred when He told the story of the Good Samaritan (Luke 10:25-37). Jesus routinely entered into the worlds of people who were typically bypassed by society.

Like Jesus, we must be intentional about entering into people's worlds. Only then can we share the gospel. Consider these questions: In the past, how often have you gone up to talk with someone from another culture who visited your church? When checking out at a grocery store, do you feel uncomfortable (and maybe avoid) getting in line behind someone from another culture? When you travel by air, do you feel uneasy about sitting next to someone who looks different from you? If a "foreigner" and his or her family have moved into your neighborhood, how do you feel about it?

Just as God is multicultural in nature, Jesus is a multicultural Savior. He said, "Go," but in today's America, you and I can still reach people of all nations without leaving our homes.

3. *Build God's kingdom on earth.* While we look forward to the glorious future our Savior has prepared for us, we can start building His kingdom right here on earth by reaching out to people of different cultures with the gospel. Review the following verses, then close your eyes and imagine what heaven will be like:

> I looked and there before me was a great multitude that no one could count, from *every nation, tribe, people and language*, standing before the throne and in front of the Lamb. They were wearing white robes and were holding palm branches in their hands. And they cried out in a loud voice: "Salvation belongs to our God, who sits on the throne, and to the Lamb." (Revelation 7:9-10, emphasis added)

Heaven will be one big multicultural community. Think about it: Your mansion might be right next to someone from Cameroon, Trinidad, Cambodia, or any of some two hundred nations on earth. In the context of cultures and people groups, the United States is more similar to what heaven will be like than is any other nation on earth! Your multicultural community is right in front of you. All you need to do is reach out.

## Be Aware of "Divine Appointments"

I often visit the Borders bookstore in Germantown, Maryland. Once while I was there, a couple of young Chinese men came in and sat at the table across from me in the café. I remembered the Chinese way of greeting people and greeted them in Mandarin. (See the section under China.) They smiled and expressed surprise that I knew how to speak their language. I confessed I knew only a few phrases, but my greeting opened the window to talk about a number of things, and I ended up inviting them to visit our church.

Colossians 4:5 instructs us, "Be wise in the way you act toward outsiders; make the most of every opportunity." Opportunities can come at any time, which is why we need to pray that the Holy Spirit will guide us and give us the wisdom to be sensitive as well as effective in our witness. I believe God sets up these "divine appointments" between us and those who do not know Him.

Let me tell you about one such divine appointment. I have conducted several training sessions at federal government institutions. On one occasion, while waiting in the reception area before a meeting, I struck up a conversation with

### When Sharing Christ with Internationals...

- Pray regularly that the Lord will provide you with opportunities to share your faith and will make you an effective witness.
- Pray for the person you witness to. (You don't have to do this during your very first meeting, but make sure you do it before and after witnessing.)
- Remember that it may take several meetings to properly witness to a person.
- Keep in mind that some people may agree with you but fear retribution from family members. Be supportive and sensitive.
- Don't assume people who call themselves Christians are believers.
- Mention facts and figures if relevant.
- Share in an interesting way. Don't make the gospel message long and boring.
- Plan and prepare well in advance.
- Be enthusiastic.
- Don't become dejected if the person doesn't seem interested or outright rejects the gospel. Your job is to witness. It is the Holy Spirit who convicts. Don't stop praying for the person.

the friendly young receptionist. I learned that Shannon (not her real name) was from Puerto Rico; she then asked about my heritage.

Soon I was able to find out that although Shannon considered herself a Christian, she did not really understand what it means to trust Christ as Savior and Lord. Shannon considered all religions to be the same. I asked if she had three minutes to spare, then I drew a diagram to help explain what Hindus, Muslims, and Buddhists believe—and how those beliefs differ from Christianity.

Shannon gave a long pause and said, "No one ever explained it to me that way before."

With the tremendous growth and presence of non-Christian religions in America in recent years, more and more seekers—including many who consider themselves Christian—have embraced a blend of markedly unscriptural, non-Christian faiths. The urgency of this situation requires that believers become equipped to share the gospel more effectively than ever before.

One of the most overlooked places where you can be a powerful witness is in your church itself. My father-in-law tells of a divine appointment God provided him one Sunday morning. A Chinese gentleman I'll call Mr. Chen walked into the church and sat in the last row. From what my father-in-law could observe, no one took initiative to talk with the visitor. At the end of the service, my father-in-law went up to introduce himself. He learned that Mr. Chen was visiting from Shanghai on a brief business trip to the United States.

Mr. Chen then said with a thick Chinese accent, "I have always been interested in Christianity. What is it all about?" My father-in-law explained the gospel to him. Mr. Chen requested a Bible and my father-in-law's e-mail address so that he could keep in touch. Mr. Chen returned to Shanghai and corresponded with my father-in-law via e-mail for several weeks. Then one day he wrote to say that he had given his life to the Lord, was reading the Bible daily, and was sharing the gospel with his family.

Imagine what would have happened if my father-in-law had not taken the step to greet Mr. Chen. But he did...and God's kingdom gained a soul for Jesus. This story could be your story. The next time you see someone of another culture in your church, take that step, keep that divine appointment, and enter into that person's world.

## WHAT DO YOU DO FOR A LIVING?

I once overheard a Christian man being asked what he did for a living. His reply: "I am an evangelist working as a banker." What an amazing attitude! Indeed, all of us have been called to be witnesses. Just substitute your vocation for the word *banker*, and make that statement your own. Write it in big bold letters in your Bible; post it on a three-by-five-inch card in your car or someplace where you'll see it every day. May it remind you of the most important calling of God in your life.

My pastor has a poster in his office that reads:

*Jesus said, "Follow me and I will make you fishers of men."*
*If you are not fishing, you are not following!*

## THE FISHERMAN ON WITNESSING

Whether we're sharing the gospel with Americans or internationals, the apostle Peter gave us some vital, fundamental guidelines for effective witnessing. Consider the big fisherman's words carefully: "But in your hearts set apart Christ as Lord. Always be prepared to give an answer to everyone who asks you to give the reason for the hope that you have. But do this with gentleness and respect" (1 Peter 3:15). I want to encourage you to keep Peter's advice in your heart as you prepare to talk with others about Jesus:

- *But in your hearts set apart Christ as Lord.* You must know Christ before you can share the gospel.
- *Always be prepared.* Be on the lookout for opportunities—divine appointments—the Holy Spirit brings your way.
- *Give an answer to everyone who asks you.* We must live in such a way that people will naturally want to know the secret of our hope and upbeat attitudes. We must also be creative in our conversations in order to create opportunities in which people can ask us about the gospel.
- *Give the reason for the hope that you have.* Be prepared to share your testimony. Start with an attention-grabbing opening. Be clear and concise, avoiding Christian jargon. Why did you become a Christian? How did it change your life?

- *But do this with gentleness and respect.* Do not discuss the gospel in an argumentative way, which only makes your listener defensive or antagonistic. And *never* make fun of someone else's religion or culture.

Think for a moment about what your life would be like if you didn't know Jesus. If you are a true believer, the very thought is frightening, isn't it? Yet millions of people across this nation are living without Him. Sadly, the number of believers isn't growing simply because we aren't sharing our faith and hope with those who don't know Him.

## BUT SHOULDN'T THEY BE THE ONES TO CONFORM TO *OUR* CULTURE?

If the United States as a country is to move forward, it has to move forward as a coordinated team. It is essential for those of us who live in this great nation to make the effort to understand one another. Stereotypes and prejudices ultimately hurt each one of us.

Some may take a look at this book and think, *Why can't foreigners just conform to our standards? They are the ones who decided to come here. Do I have to do all this? After all, if I love beef and pork, do I have to give it up because I am trying to reach my Hindu, Buddhist, or Muslim friend?*

The point is that we don't have to give up anything. We simply must try to make it easy for a person to relate to us and consider the gospel of Jesus Christ. If something should act as an impediment, let's remove it *during the time* we are interacting with our international friend. The apostle Paul said it well in his letter to the Roman Christians:

Therefore let us stop passing judgment on one another. Instead, make up your mind *not to put any stumbling block or obstacle in your brother's way.* As one who is in the Lord Jesus, I am fully convinced that no food is unclean in itself. But if anyone regards something as unclean, then for him it is unclean. If your brother is distressed because of what you eat, you are no longer acting in love. Do not by your eating destroy your brother for whom Christ died. (Romans 14:13-15, emphasis added)

If your eating beef or pork is likely to cause your Hindu, Buddhist, or Muslim friend to shut out the gospel, then forsaking these foods in the presence of your friend is not only the courteous thing to do, it also removes a potential barrier to his or her consideration of Jesus Christ. One of my wife's high-school friends is a Hindu and a vegetarian for religious reasons. Whenever she is at our house for a meal, we simply cook a vegetarian meal. We also have a close relationship with a Muslim family, and we often share meals with them. During such occasions, we simply avoid pork. We do these things out of respect for our international friends and to avoid placing a stumbling block in the way of a potential relationship with Jesus Christ.

## AMERICA: A MELTING POT?

My wife and I once visited a beautiful Pennsylvania bed-and-breakfast operated by a Mennonite family. While we were there we noticed four or five ladies working on an exquisitely crafted quilt. They were all working from different directions, but the design was forming a beautiful and unified pattern. That is precisely my impression of America. Some refer to the United States as a melting pot, but I prefer to believe it is like a quilt of great workmanship. The fabric of different cultures and ethnicities joins together to make an attractive mosaic. After all, that is what makes this nation so great: the contribution each immigrant and his or her descendants have made, and will continue to make, to the unique fabric of America.

People from other religions and cultures now live, study, and work among us. They are America's most overlooked mission field. We cannot make excuses anymore. The eternal destinies of millions are at stake.

Remember: *If you are not fishing, you are not following!*

# 3

# Dispelling Cultural Myths, Stereotypes, and Prejudices

India has a wealth of stories. Countless folk tales, myths, and legends have survived a history of over five thousand years of civilization. As a young kid growing up in Calcutta, India, I pestered my grandmother and my many aunts to tell me stories. I devoured magazines, comics, and books featuring interesting and intriguing tales. Most, if not all, of them contained a valuable nugget of truth or moral lesson. One story I recall strikes me as relevant to the context of this book.

In a remote village in northern India among the foothills of the Himalayas, there lived six blind men. One day a man with an elephant came to the village. There was much excitement in the village, for it had been a long time since anyone had seen an elephant. The news reached the six blind men. They talked among themselves and discovered that none of them had ever encountered an elephant.

"We have to go and figure out what this elephant is like," said one blind man. "We have heard so much about this animal, and we may never get a chance to do this again."

His companions agreed. So the six blind men made their way to the center of the village where the elephant was being kept. When they arrived the animal was sitting down. The first blind man walked up to the elephant and patted its massive body and hard skin. After a few moments he walked away and said, "I don't know what all this fuss is about. An elephant is just like a wall!"

The second blind man walked up to the elephant and felt its trunk. Then he said, "No, my friend, you've got it wrong. An elephant is just like a snake!"

The elephant stood up just as the third blind man approached. He felt one of the elephant's legs and announced, "Both of you are wrong. An elephant is just like a tree!"

The fourth blind man touched the elephant's ear and said, "You are wrong. I think the elephant is just like a fan!"

The fifth blind man felt the elephant's tusk and told the others, "The elephant is just like a spear!"

The sixth blind man felt the elephant's tail and said, "You are all wrong. The elephant is just like a rope!"

Each of the six blind men took his limited experience with an elephant and imposed it upon his view of what the entire animal must look like.

The point is this: Stereotypes happen when we take one or two experiences with a member of a group and apply our impressions to the whole group. Suppose you have a bad experience with someone from India. Chances are you will think *all* Indians are the same.

As the United States moves from a homogeneous society to a heterogeneous one, it is becoming more and more imperative for Christians to become competent in cross-cultural ministry, communication, and living. Furthermore, the influx of people of so many different religions, especially over the last twenty years, makes it more important for us to be effective witnesses for our Lord.

First, let's tackle the issue of how stereotypes form. It is a process. In my cross-cultural training with corporate America, I often start by asking people to list some common stereotypes they have of Indians (since I am originally from India, I can get away with poking good-hearted fun at my compatriots!). The same answers—even ones that are contradictory—seem to show up repeatedly:

- Indians are Hindus.
- Indians don't eat cows.
- Indians own the Dunkin' Donuts chain stores.

- Most Indians are computer programmers.
- Most Indians are doctors.
- Most Indians are sales clerks at 7-Eleven stores.
- Most Indians work at gas stations.
- Indians are short and dark skinned.
- Indians are tall and fair skinned.
- Indians burn incense sticks.
- Indians eat really hot and spicy food.
- Indians have a thicker accent than most Asians.
- Indians don't have as thick an accent as other Asians.

The list goes on. When we take a look at some of these stereotypes, we realize that people often translate their experience with one or a few Indians into what all Indians must be like. In reality, India is probably the world's most diverse nation.

Take, for instance, the stereotype that Indians are Hindus. That is true for 82 percent of the population. But India also has a large Muslim minority and a significant number of Christians, Sikhs, Buddhists, and Jains.

In order to counter the stereotypical responses to internationals, we need to understand the process by which our impressions are formed. The process has four stages, and most people don't go beyond the second stage.

## STAGE ONE: FORMING PERCEPTIONS

Jason, a twenty-something young man from Liberia, came to the United States in the early 1980s. His first job was with a major packaging company. When he reported for duty the first day, his supervisor asked him, "So where are you from?"

"I am from Liberia, sir," Jason replied, eager to please his new boss.

"Liberia, huh? I read somewhere that people in Liberia live in trees. Must have been pretty tough, climbing up and down for every little thing."

Jason laughed when he told me about this interaction, but the supervisor's response was highly stereotypical. He read *somewhere* that some Liberians lived in trees, so he assumed *all* Liberians must live in trees.

Many of us in this society grew up in a homogeneous setting and associated with people who were mostly like us. Some of us are uncomfortable with the changing face of America, with the differences we see and often do not understand in other people.

Then comes the actual experience—a couple of good, bad, or unusual experiences with a few members of a group. Or maybe we simply read something in a magazine or see something on television. We take that limited knowledge and apply it to the entire group: *If one person from a group behaves, talks, or thinks in a certain way, then everyone else must also behave, talk, or think that way.*

The great danger in this type of thinking is clear, as no two individuals are completely alike. We need to relate to people without letting our past perceptions cloud our judgment just because someone has a certain skin color, hails from a certain country, or holds certain religious beliefs.

We often let our perceptions go unchallenged by overstating differences and downplaying similarities between ourselves and those who are different from us. At the same time, we overstate similarities and downplay differences between ourselves and those who are more like us.

The net result is that we tend to *drift toward* people who are like us and *drift away* from people who are different from us. Consider this: If your church offers an opportunity to interact with other believers before or after the Sunday morning service, do people tend to stay within their groups or do they reach out and interact *meaningfully* with people from all groups? If an international were to step inside your church, would he or she feel welcome? How many people besides the greeters and ushers would actually talk to that visitor?

Regardless of our backgrounds, we are all different and similar in many ways. Consider the Myers-Briggs Personality Type Indicator test, which divides the human race into sixteen personality types. Research has shown this test to be highly accurate, and it is extensively used in corporate America. When administered to white men and Chinese women, it was found that a white man and a Chinese woman who had the same personality type approached problems in more or less the same way. Personality played a bigger role than demographics in how people reacted to different situations.

Think for a moment about Jesus' lifestyle. Our Lord was a champion of cross-cultural ministry, shattering prejudices along the way. When Jesus called Matthew to be His follower, the tax collector immediately left his lucrative career. Later, while Jesus was having dinner at Matthew's house, many tax collectors and sinners ate with Him. The Pharisees grumbled, "Why does your teacher eat with tax collectors and 'sinners'?" (Matthew 9:11).

These people were the bypassed. They did not belong; they were outside the group. In Jesus' eyes, their income, profession, status in society, education, race, or ethnicity did not matter. Only one thing mattered—the fact that God loved them and, without Jesus, they were lost.

## STAGE TWO: DEVELOPING STEREOTYPES

When perceptions and assumptions go unchallenged, they can crystallize into stereotypes. This happens when we make generalizations based on improper evidence. In the midst of the information deluge that we are subjected to on a daily basis, it is natural and often practical to categorize huge amounts of complicated data. However, in terms of human experience, we tend to use stereotypical responses as a mechanism to block true assessments of individuals or events. We may even systematically screen out any evidence that might contradict that stereotype.

First, let's try to define stereotypes. Perhaps one of the best definitions is found in Marilyn Loden and Judith Rosener's groundbreaking book, *Workforce America*. The authors define a stereotype as "a fixed and distorted generalization made about all members of a particular group; a rigid judgment which doesn't take into account the here and now."

Have you ever heard someone say, "It's a male thing" or "It's a female thing"? Such phrases are an easy way to explain a gender behavior, even though we *know* not all men or women would behave in that manner. Sometimes stereotypes are dangerous, and sometimes they're harmless. When Ed, a foreign student from Ghana, came to the United States, he encountered a stereotypical response right at the customs checkpoint at JFK airport. The customs official was no doubt trying to be amiable when he said to Ed, "So, do you folks still use bullock carts as your main form of transportation? Flying must be quite a thrill."

Ed just smiled. This customs official must have read an article or seen a television report that portrayed Ghanaians using bullock carts as a form of transportation. In his mind he had imposed that single incident on the entire country of Ghana. Of course, it was probably done at the subconscious level. We must strive to avoid such generalizations if we are to effectively reach people of other cultures. We must constantly keep in mind that individuals are different from one another—in other nations, just as they are in America. Yes, there may be customs and traditions that hold true for entire groups, but more often than not, stereotypes simply inhibit our ability to get to know people on a close, individual basis.

Jesus was highly critical of the Pharisees. Yet when Nicodemus came to meet Him, Jesus' response to him was open and engaging. (See John 3:1-12.) Just because most Pharisees were hypocrites did not mean *all* of them were corrupt. Jesus did not let His opinion of Pharisees cloud His interaction with a man who genuinely sought the truth.

The danger is that most stereotypes do not happen at the conscious level. However, when confronted with facts to the contrary, most people will at least consider the alternative as long as they have not allowed their stereotypes to become prejudices.

## STAGE THREE: BECOMING PREJUDICED

When you link someone's ethnicity with an unfavorable characteristic, you reveal your prejudice. For instance, in the weeks following the terrorist attacks of September 11, 2001, there were more than one thousand recorded incidents of attacks on people who physically resembled Arabs (and this included South Asians). The people who initiated these attacks took one characteristic of some deviant souls and linked it with every person who, in their judgment, looked Middle Eastern. Thankfully, the majority of Americans are not guilty of such narrow-minded thinking, but prejudices do indeed exist.

I was at a Christian wedding reception when I encountered an ugly form of prejudicial response from a Christian lady. After the wonderful and God-honoring ceremony, all of us who were in attendance made our way to the reception hall, which was in the basement of the church.

Along with my wife, Erika, my mother-in-law, and three friends, I got food from the buffet table and found a place for us to sit. We settled at a round table, with one chair remaining empty. Soon, a middle-aged lady I'll call Joanne asked if she could sit with us. We said yes and immediately started introducing ourselves to her. After the introductions, Joanne looked at me and asked, "So where are *you* from?"

"I live in Maryland, but I am originally from India," I replied.

Joanne made a face and said, "India! Well, I can tell you India has the world's worst human rights record!"

Somewhat taken aback I responded, "You mean India has a worse human rights record than China, Cuba, Rwanda, Liberia, Sudan, and several other nations that have been declared by Amnesty International as among the worst—and in which India does not figure, certainly not in the top?"

"I don't care what Amnesty says," she retorted. "I *know* India is the worst!"

"May I ask what makes you say so?" I queried.

"Well," Joanne said, "I have seen photographs of what you people are doing to folks in Kashmir."

Notice how she went from "India" to "you people." In her mind every Indian was guilty of committing atrocities against the people of Kashmir—including me! The conversation became increasingly tense as I tried to provide logical arguments as to why her premise was wrong. Kashmir represents a volatile and highly charged political issue between India and Pakistan. A proxy war is going on at the border almost every day. Sporadic violence in the region has claimed many lives. While the Kashmir issue is beyond the scope of this book, the fact is that historically, socially, and politically, this one topic is highly sensitive to most Indians and Pakistanis.

"How do you know the photographs taken were from India?" I continued. "They could have been taken in another country. It could have been anywhere."

"I know because I work for the CIA," she replied.

I wondered what the CIA would have to say about that!

"Have you ever been to India?" I asked.

"No."

"Have you ever been outside the United States?"

"No."

"Have you seen any evidence other than that alleged by the photographs?"

"No, but I *know* India has the worst human rights record."

At this juncture I realized that no matter how convincing my arguments, this person was not interested in a rational assessment of the situation. She had made up her mind, and no one was going to dissuade her from her prejudicial position. It wasn't long before people from our table started making excuses to go and visit with other friends and acquaintances in the room.

If I were not a Christian, and if this had been my first interaction with a Christian, I would be hard pressed to believe anything about Christianity. As Christians, when we interact with people from other cultures and religions, we need to keep in mind the appropriateness of what we talk about—at least until we get to know a person better. That's why I will provide you with several pointers in the next section about safe topics to talk about and sensitive topics to avoid when interacting with internationals.

When we believe so strongly in stereotypes, we, in effect, become prejudiced. We believe so strongly in our opinions that no matter what kind of evidence is presented to us, we will not change our minds.

## STAGE FOUR: EMBRACING ETHNOCENTRISM

Ethnocentrism is the belief that one's own race is superior to all others. In varying degrees some form of ethnocentrism is ingrained in most cultures of the world. Some traditions reinforce it in the minds of people within a certain group. However, when this kind of thinking pervades every aspect of our lives, we enter into a category of what I call *extreme ethnocentrism,* which says that "my race, culture, color, gender, and so on are better than yours. Period." An extreme example of this is the Nazi regime. If you read Adolf Hitler's *Mein Kampf,* you will find page after page of extreme ethnocentrism.

In our society people in this category make up a small number. But they are there. Unfortunately, some are Christians and others call themselves Christian.

One of the greatest examples of Jesus' attitudes and thoughts on prejudice and ethnocentrism is found in John 4, which we mentioned in the last chapter. Jesus was tired after a long walk, so He sat down by a well. A Samaritan woman came to draw water and Jesus asked, "Will you give me a drink?" (verse 7).

The incident in itself may not sound unusual. But the fact was that Jews hated Samaritans. Jesus, however, had no cultural reservations. His conversation with the Samaritan woman revealed that no matter what our background, culture, or race, our Lord sees us as all the same. Should we do any less?

## ARROGANCE OR IGNORANCE?

We have been talking about how we can avoid stereotypical responses to people of other cultures. But as we strive to do so, there is the distinct possibility that *we* might be stereotyped by people of other cultures. What should we do then?

Often, when faced with a stereotypical response, we attribute it to either arrogance or ignorance. Our reaction will pretty much depend upon how we perceive it. Let me explain with two examples.

I actually witnessed the following episode. Hamid, a tourist from Pakistan, enters a busy fast-food restaurant. He looks at the menu on the board and orders a burger combo meal. The elderly lady behind the counter takes the order and asks, "Here or to go?" She says this so quickly that the words run together.

Hamid is totally perplexed. He replies, "I am here to buy food and eat."

At this point, the busy lady can offer one of two responses.

1. *Arrogance.* She could think, *Is this fellow trying to act smart?* She will probably repeat the question and get the same answer. She will then say something like, "What's with the wisecrack? Can't you give a simple answer to a simple question?"

2. *Ignorance.* She could think, *He looks like he is not from here. Maybe I should explain.* She will then say, "I'm sorry—I should have explained. I wanted to know whether you would like to eat your food here or take it with you to go."

In this real-life incident, the lady chose the first response.

Then let's consider the example of Mr. Mokito, who has arrived as a tourist in Orlando. He is staying with his family at a hotel. The housekeeper comes around, and Mr. Mokito holds up his shoes to her and says, "Please shine my shoes before you go."

What do you think will happen? Again, one of two responses from the housekeeper are possible:

1. *Arrogance.* She could think, *What nerve! How dare he?* This would attribute Mr. Mokito's request to arrogance, and you can bet there would be problems.

2. *Ignorance.* She could think, *This may happen in his culture, and he probably doesn't know that we don't do that here in America.* This would attribute Mr. Mokito's request to ignorance. She would then try to explain to Mr. Mokito why she cannot shine his shoes.

You can see the difference. When we attribute someone's stereotypical remark to ignorance, we are more inclined to give the benefit of the doubt and explain ourselves. If, on the other hand, we assume the other person is being arrogant, we are likely to respond in kind. So the next time you face a situation in which someone from another culture or religious background makes a stereotypical remark or request, assume innocent ignorance. Take the time to patiently explain yourself. Chances are, the true reason behind the situation is ignorance.

Remember: First come our perceptions that lead to stereotypes, if unchallenged. When we start to believe strongly in stereotypes, we become prejudiced. An extreme form of prejudicial thinking is exclusive ethnocentrism.

Fortunately, most Christians have not advanced through all four of the stages.

Yet, when it comes to responding or reaching out to people of other cultures, we do tend to gravitate toward one of seven common responses. We will explore these responses in the next chapter, but for now, the bottom line is this: When we judge people on the basis of their race or ethnicity, we miss the point. The great divide is not between people of different races, but between believers and nonbelievers!

# 4

# A Change in Attitude

I once read an interesting story about a Japanese businessman who was visiting his American counterpart in New York City. During the evening rush hour, they headed for the underground metro to catch the 4:37 train.

The American businessman started running and yelled out, "We better hurry. The next train is not until 4:49!"

The Japanese businessman calmly replied, "And what earth-shaking achievement are you planning to accomplish within those twelve minutes?"

This brief interaction reveals much about the American mind-set. Internationals generally see Americans as friendly people who sincerely try to understand their ways and culture but are often hurried and harried. Because we're so rushed, we don't invest time to truly listen and deepen our understanding.

As I have studied our interactions with people of other cultures, I have observed that we tend to give one of seven responses. Some of us may even mix a few. For Christians seeking to build cross-cultural friendships, it is critical to identify which responses typify our mind-set because, as you will see, only one of the seven is the practically effective, biblically correct response.

## Pretenders: "I Don't Have the Time!"
Internationals quickly learn that when someone asks "How are you doing today?" the speaker isn't really interested in the answer. *Pretenders* tend to approach internationals with the same superficial attitude. That is, they may be

serious about their faith, family, career, and life goals, but getting to know internationals isn't one of those goals. They tend to be Day-Timer people who don't like interruptions in their schedule. They are cordial to internationals but would rather not get close. They may see internationals as people who may well become a burden. So why bother? Plus, they just don't have the time.

A typical Pretender will think, *I guess I should get to know these foreigners in my church and neighborhood, but I don't have the time, and honestly, I don't know if I care.* Pretenders also get impatient with internationals because the clock moves a lot slower in other countries. This is a hard lesson to learn for our microwave society.

Pretenders need to remember that the chief way God communicates the gospel to internationals in America is through His human agents—otherwise known as Christians. What Pretenders may see as an interruption in their daily schedule may be a divine appointment set by God.

It is wise to reflect on how Jesus handled interruptions. Even a cursory study of the Gospels reveals that a huge number of people constantly disrupted Jesus' plans…or so it seems. The fact is, God wants us to put people first, not simply engage in a lifelong quest to build a bigger pile of perishable goods.

*Pretenders…*

- approach internationals with a superficial attitude
- would like to get to know internationals but simply can't seem to make the time
- believe it is better to be cordial rather than close to internationals
- don't like to have their schedules interrupted

## DODGERS: "ARE THEY SAFE?"

*Dodgers* are greatly concerned about their personal safety. Of course, trying to ensure safety is one of the great modern trends. People like to live in gated communities, have an alarm system in their cars, and burglar-proof their homes. There is nothing wrong with that. However, for some people the quest for safety can take extreme forms, where anything out of the ordinary is a calamity waiting to happen.

Several years ago, a Korean student became lost in northern California. Without much thought, this young man knocked at the door of a suburban home to ask for directions. Before he had a chance to knock again, the owner of the house shot him dead. This sad story may seem extreme, but things like this do happen.

A more subtle form of this attitude takes place every Sunday in churches across America. A Dodger sees a foreigner and intentionally stays away. No matter what happens, a Dodger will not interact with internationals. His thinking goes this way: We don't know their culture. Who knows where they are from or what diseases they may be carrying?

*Dodgers...*
- shy away from foreigners
- are wary of people they are not familiar with
- feel it is better to stick with people of their own culture—with their own circle of friends
- are greatly (and sometimes overly) concerned about their personal safety

Dodgers are not necessarily obsessive-compulsive people, but they tend to be wary of anyone they are not familiar with. It is, of course, prudent to be wary of strangers, but Dodgers feel it is better to stick to one's own culture and one's own circle of friends.

People who typically respond in this way need to realize that God is the Creator of languages and cultures. It was at the Tower of Babel that God created the many languages of the world. He also scattered the people to different parts of the earth, thus creating new cultures. Dodgers also need to realize that every human being has been created in the image of God Himself, and when we mistreat or devalue another person, we risk mistreating or devaluing God.

## Globalizers: "All Cultures Are the Same"

*Globalizers* believe people are the same everywhere, and to some extent that is true. People do have similar needs and wants. But as we have seen, people from different cultures have different traditions and customs. Ignoring these traditions or belittling them only makes people feel disregarded and disrespected.

Globalizers are often friendly people. They are among the first to introduce themselves to a person of another culture who is in their church or social setting. The problem is, they do not validate the uniqueness of each culture. The road to a meaningful relationship with someone of another culture is a slow but rewarding one that requires two-way listening and learning. People from other cultures are usually eager to understand the traditions and customs of the American culture. They are eager to fit in. If we want to broaden our own knowledge base and have meaningful relationships, we must be sure that the learning happens both ways.

*Globalizers...*
- are friendly people
- believe all cultures are the same
- can often greatly insult or embarrass someone from another culture by saying or doing something inappropriate
- are not good listeners

The biggest problem with Globalizers is that they can seem very indifferent to the beliefs and customs of other cultures. An example would be taking a Hindu friend for a burger or inviting a Muslim friend for a dinner of pork chops. (Hindus don't eat beef, and Muslims don't eat pork.) Globalizers either do not know enough about other cultures, or they simply do not believe it is necessary to regard foreign customs with respect.

Globalizers need to realize that there is incredible richness in the diversity of God's creation, including the diversity of cultures. Of course, this doesn't mean we have to lose our own identities or nod to unbiblical statements. Our job is threefold: (1) Respect the other person's beliefs and customs without compromising our own Christian principles; (2) be ready to share the gospel gently and respectfully when the opportunity arrives; and (3) be a true friend.

## PATRONIZERS: "WE KNOW BEST!"

Zageer was an international student from the small Himalayan Hindu kingdom of Nepal. He was attending a Christian college because he had heard that faith-based schools were safer and friendlier than their secular counterparts. But after two years of study, he transferred to another college, totally disgusted with the attitude of Christians toward him.

*Patronizers...*

- often approach internationals with a we-know-best mentality
- believe internationals must be saved any possible way, by any possible means
- can be very insistent when sharing the gospel, and they get annoyed when internationals do not share their views
- often see internationals as somewhat less than them

What had happened? It seems almost everyone on campus knew he wasn't a Christian, so several people shared the gospel with him. On many occasions people would pressure him to make a decision right away. In another instance a professor gave an assignment to his class to interview a non-Christian and find out about his or her worldview. Zageer was besieged with students wanting to know about his religion and telling him why his beliefs were wrong. One student even went so far as to say, "How can you be so silly to believe in multiple gods?" Furthermore, Zageer also received a note from the financial aid department saying that many of the school's scholarships were restricted to Christians. Apart from the exit interview, no one made any serious attempt to contact him after he transferred.

*Patronizers* are not mean-spirited people. In fact, they believe strongly that the gospel needs to be communicated with internationals at every opportunity. They want internationals to be saved. The problem is that they often convey a we-know-best attitude that regards people from other cultures as somewhat less than them. This usually is not an outright declaration, but a subconscious belief that internationals are less informed or less intelligent.

When sharing the gospel, Patronizers can become insistent and annoyed when an international does not agree with their viewpoint. They need to realize that people who come to this country are often among the brightest and best in their homeland. They also need to know that a Christian's job is simply to communicate the gospel. It is the Holy Spirit who convicts a person. We do not have the power to save anyone; only Jesus Christ can.

## CATEGORIZERS: "ONE GOOD OR BAD EXPERIENCE IS ENOUGH"

*Categorizers* love to put others into neatly divided compartments. This makes it easier for them to deal with (and sometimes cope with) certain characteristics of people they don't know well.

When it comes to internationals, Categorizers consider one experience—no matter how isolated—with a person of one culture as the standard for evaluating everyone from that particular culture. This is the most common of all responses. Say you have a singular, unique experience with someone from Kenya. If you are a Categorizer, you will evaluate everyone from Kenya based on that experience.

My wife and I attended Eastern University in Philadelphia. The school had students from forty countries, and we were friends with almost all of them. We got married right after our graduation, and many of the foreign students from Eastern were invited to the wedding. We had an interesting situation with a student from a certain African nation. When he arrived, he came with several of his friends *who had not been invited.* This greatly stressed my mother-in-law, but Erika and I were amused as our friend told us it was their custom to bring all their friends and acquaintances to a wedding ceremony. Weeks later, when we met another friend from the same country, we shared the incident with him and he reacted indignantly, "That may be the custom in *his* tribe, but it is certainly not in *ours!*"

We learned that, of a dozen major tribes in this particular country, only one tribe practiced that custom. If not corrected by our friend, we would have assumed that everyone in that country brought uninvited friends to weddings.

That is the danger of categorizing. The human mind likes to categorize because it makes things simpler and easier to remember. However, when we view one good, bad, or unique experience as typical, we enter into the danger zone of stereotyping—of compartmentalizing people into our preconceived (and often ill-conceived) ideas.

*Categorizers…*
- exhibit the most common of all responses toward internationals
- love to fit things and people into tidy compartments
- usually base their ideas about a specific culture on one good, bad, or unique experience in the past
- usually have pet phrases such as "It's a male thing"

Categorizers need to realize that Jesus did not believe in stereotypes. He interacted with people as individuals rather than as parts of homogeneous groups. There are many examples of this in the Gospels. His meeting with the woman at the well was a blow to the stereotype people had of Samaritans. Furthermore, even though He was so strongly opposed to the Pharisees, His conversation with the Pharisee Nicodemus gave us one of the best-loved chapters in the Gospels.

We must see people as unique individuals rather than trying to fit them into an ideology born of past experiences.

### XENOPHOBES: "NOT IN MY NEIGHBORHOOD!"

If you live in any neighborhood in Asia, Africa, or Latin America, chances are that people within at least a quarter-mile radius know you very well. In a collectivist society, people live in communities where everyone knows everyone.

Western society is, of course, individualistic. People have their circle of friends, but these often do not include their neighbors. It is not unusual to find Americans who know nothing about their neighbors across the street or down the block. Of course, American society is highly mobile, and this doesn't help create communities where people know one another well.

The news media have done a great job (if you want to call it that) of presenting stories of ex-convicts and violent criminals who move into respectable communities. Although rare in terms of statistics, this has led to a fear of strangers. Don't get me wrong. I will be the first one to say personal safety should be a top priority, especially for those with children. But when we lock ourselves in our homes and refuse to communicate with anybody we do not know, then there is a problem.

*Xenophobes...*

- dislike and are very wary of people who are not of their culture
- deliberately stay away from internationals in every situation
- sometimes find it difficult to cross over the great divide of skin color
- find it very hard to accept the transformation of America into a multicultural society

*Xenophobes* have a persistent fear of strangers. Many of them have grown up in a homogeneous society and dislike the fact that the American culture is becoming more multicultural by the day. They would rather move away from people who are not like them. They rarely take steps to get to know someone of another culture. In social or church settings, they tend to drift away from people of other cultures and congregate in groups that are homogeneous in nature. What's more, they seem unable to cross the great divide of skin color and cultural differences.

An extreme form of xenophobia is exclusive ethnocentrism, which espouses the belief that one's culture is superior to all others. (See chapter 3.) This is not patriotism. It is an active conviction that skin color or cultural affiliation bestows upon humans distinctive qualities. This was the conviction that drove the Nazi regime and led to World War II.

Xenophobes need to realize that the great divide is not among people of different skin colors, nor is it among people of different cultural or ethnic backgrounds. The great divide is between believers and unbelievers. It is our job to bridge this divide by reaching out in friendship and sharing the good news of salvation.

## EMPATHIZERS: "WE ARE ALL PRECIOUS IN GOD'S SIGHT"

Of the seven responses discussed in this chapter, this is the one that is both biblically correct and practically effective. *Empathizers* recognize that every human being, regardless of skin color or ethnic origin, is created in the image of God and is precious to Him.

Empathizers reach out to internationals just as they would to any other person. They do not let the filter of preconceived ideas skew their perceptions. They know people all over the world have similar needs and wants and that one of their greatest needs is to connect with other people. Empathizers are culturally sensitive. They do not denigrate other people's customs or traditions. They are learners who listen well.

*Empathizers...*
- believe all people are created equal and are precious to God
- are culturally sensitive
- are learners who listen well
- know that learning about other cultures will broaden their own perspectives

Jesus was a great Empathizer. He did not let prevalent cultural leanings cloud His interaction with people. He was compassionate toward people who were bypassed, ignored, or hated by society. These included women, tax collectors, and the diseased. If He were walking the earth today, He would reach out to every cultural cross section of our society. How can we do any less?

### How to Become an Empathizer

If you see even a little bit of yourself in any of the first six categories, you might want to reevaluate your response to our biblical mandate to reach people from every tribe and nation—especially when they happen to be right in your own neighborhood. Many of the attitudes against certain cultures are ingrained at community or societal levels. However, to bring about a change at the societal level, we must start with ourselves. Here is a simple graph to illustrate how a change in attitude can start with the individual and spark the imagination of a whole nation:

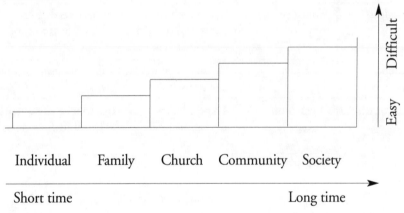

We have the power to change America. Think what would happen if Christian values and principles were practiced in every home, school, institution, corporation, and governmental institution in America. We could bring about a societal change the likes of which the world has never seen. This could happen if every Christian took seriously the job of telling others the good news of Jesus Christ. Change starts at the individual and family level and then impacts the society in general.

If you find yourself in a category other than the Empathizers, what can you do? What do you do when you notice people in your circle of friends (or small group or church) who sport attitudes that clearly do not belong in the Empathizer group?

First of all, check your own thinking. Do you place people in stereotypical compartments? Do you make categorizing statements such as "It's a male thing"? Do you let one good, bad, or unique experience with a person from a different culture shape your opinion of everyone from that culture? Do you see internationals as somewhat inferior or backward? Do you avoid people of other cultures?

Here's a quick snapshot of the six ineffective responses to internationals and some ways you can change this kind of thinking:

| Type | Typical Response | Change in Attitude |
|------|-----------------|--------------------|
| Pretenders | Uninvolved | Human interruptions can be divine appointments. |
| Dodgers | Avoidance | People everywhere have similar needs and wants. One of their greatest needs is to connect with other people. |
| Globalizers | Insensitive | Different cultures have different customs and traditions. |
| Patronizers | Ostentatious | Those who come into this country are often among the brightest and best in their own countries. |
| Categorizers | Stereotypical | A single (or a few) good, bad, or unique experience(s) with one culture may not be a common characteristic of people from that culture. |
| Xenophobes | Prejudicial | The great divide is not between people of different skin color or national origin, but between believers and unbelievers. |

## RELATING TO INTERNATIONALS NEW TO AMERICA

One of the best times to build a relationship with internationals is when they first arrive in the United States. They are new, they are eager to learn, and they are homesick. Many who come from collectivist societies have a hard time figuring out how people in this society can live such isolated lives without a community. This is precisely where the church can fill a great void. The church can become their community. However, we need to remember some guidelines when relating to new arrivals.

1. Use simple English and short sentences. Avoid big words.

2. Keep your greeting formal. Refer to the other person by his or her title and last name. In some countries, calling a person by his or her first name is practiced only among family members and close friends.

3. Speak slowly and don't shout. People from other cultures who have just recently come to the United States generally have a hard time understanding the American accent. If the person appears confused, write down what you have to say. They can often understand written English better than spoken English.

4. Make a special effort to find out if the other person has understood what you have said. Ask the person to repeat what you just told them to make sure he or she clearly understood what you said.

5. Respect silence. If the person is quiet in the midst of your conversation, it doesn't mean he or she has finished talking. In many cultures people pause frequently while talking to think over what has been said or what they might want to say. Don't rush to fill short pauses.

6. Restate your point with different words if necessary. Many American and Christian slang words are gibberish to internationals. Avoid slang and Christian buzzwords.

7. Show interest by asking questions and listening to the answers.

8. Keep in mind that certain behaviors we take for granted in this country could be considered a sign of rudeness or inattentiveness. For instance, chewing gum or whistling, especially in church, can be considered impolite.

9. Practice the Golden Rule: Do unto others as you would have them do unto you. This is especially true in the realm of religion or national origin. What you may think is a great joke about a certain country or religion may actually come across as bigotry. Never ridicule the traditional beliefs or customs of another country or religion.

10. Use gestures. Utilize your hands and body language to express yourself. But avoid using gestures that people from other cultures might consider offensive. (These gestures are discussed in the following chapters.)

11. Don't rush the person. The clock moves a lot slower in many foreign countries. Be patient and allow the other person to take the time to express him- or herself.

12. Be careful about touching. For instance, although hugs are commonly accepted as a form of greeting in an American church setting, they may not be considered appropriate for someone from another culture.

13. Keep in mind that people who come to the United States from other countries are among the best and brightest in their homeland. They often have to deal with several culture-shock issues such as different kinds of food, clothing, customs, financial worries, and homesickness. Be sensitive.

14. Above all, practice the universal code for instilling reassurance in a fellow human being: Smile!

Part 2

# Fulfilling the Great Commission in Our Neighborhoods

# 5

# General Guidelines
# for Cross-Cultural Interaction

Before you begin interacting with people of other cultures, you need to understand some basic principles about people from other countries. This section provides several general guidelines that will help you effectively relate—and eventually witness—to internationals.

Before we get into specifics, let's make one thing clear: The guidelines presented here are *general* and apply in *most* circumstances. In your interactions you may find that some people are exceptions. That's because it is impossible to come up with a set of rules that apply to everyone from a particular culture. Use these guidelines, but be open to learning more about your international friend.*

## Keys to Effective Cross-Cultural Interaction

Following are twenty-one keys to being effective in your interactions with people from other cultures and religions:

1. *Get to know your international friend before sharing your faith.* Unless you feel prompted by the Spirit and feel you will never have a second chance, don't get into religion right away when interacting with an international. One of the

---

\* Most statistics in part 2 of this book are taken from *The World Almanac and Book of Facts, 2002* (New York: World Almanac Books, 2001).

biggest complaints from people of other religions in this country is that Christians are constantly telling them they need to "get saved." But these same Christians are not at all interested in them otherwise.

Some wise person once said, "People will not care how much you know unless they know how much you care." First, get to know your international friend. Second, get to know what he or she believes. Third, share the gospel. All three steps can take place in a single setting, or it may be spread over several meetings. The point is, be sensitive and avoid arguments. (See part 3 of this book for specific pointers.)

2. *Keep in mind that time is often relative.* You've heard that "time is money." But for most of the world the clock moves a lot more slowly than in the United States. It is not unusual for people from Asian, Latin American, and African countries to be late for appointments. In many countries in these regions, it is *customary* to arrive late. Two important exceptions are Korea and Japan, where people tend to arrive *earlier* than the appointed time.

Keep in mind that this applies mostly to newly arrived internationals or first-generation immigrants rather than to those who were born in the United States. Still, you should try to be on time. Also, don't get impatient with internationals who may seem to take longer to do things than the time you are accustomed to. Maybe it's a reminder that you need to slow down!

---

### Attitudes About Time Are Different Around the World

- Time is money. (American proverb)
- Everything must wait its turn…peach blossoms for the second month and chrysanthemums for the ninth. (Japanese proverb)
- Those who rush arrive first at the grave. (Spanish proverb)
- The future belongs to him who knows how to wait. (Russian proverb)
- The clock did not invent the man. (Nigerian proverb)
- There is summer and there is winter; what is the need for hurry? (Turkish proverb)

3. *Learn what yes and no mean.* In many cultures it is considered rude to say no. In some countries, especially Japan, people may go to extraordinary lengths to avoid saying no. You have to be creative and perceptive in order to understand whether your international friend really means yes or no. For instance, suppose you invite a Japanese friend to a church event and he says, "Good." In order to find out whether he truly wants to attend, you will have to ask questions that don't require a no answer. You could ask, "What are you doing on Sunday morning?" The problem is, if your Japanese friend cannot say no and is not interested in coming, he may simply not show up and then avoid you completely in the future.

4. *Ask the right questions.* Never ask an international, "Do you understand?" The answer will invariably be yes. A better approach is to ask the person to tell you what he or she thinks.

5. *Recognize the potential effects of praise and criticism.* In some cultures it is highly uncomfortable for a person to receive praise and highly humiliating to receive criticism. Couch these gently and avoid giving lengthy praises or criticism in front of others. If you are criticizing, allow the other person to save face.

6. *Avoid using idiomatic phrases.* When talking to internationals, avoid idiomatic phrases. A simple greeting like "Top of the day to you" or "What's up?" can totally confuse a person. Bottom line: If your international friend looks confused after you've said something, consider whether you have just used an idiomatic phrase.

7. *Learn the best way to address your international friend.* In most cultures the use of first names is reserved for close friends and family members. A safe bet is to use titles unless you are asked not to do so. You should certainly avoid using a first name when addressing your international friend's parents or other elders in his or her house. Use Mr. or Mrs. with the last name.

8. *When you suggest getting together with your international friend, be prepared for an unexpected visit.* In some cultures close friends are welcome to drop in at any time without a prior appointment. So if you have just formed a friendship with someone who is from such a culture, you might end up saying, "Let's get together." An innocent remark, but be prepared to hear a knock at your door at

any time over the next few days. Your new friend may drop in without letting you know in advance. This is completely acceptable in his or her culture.

Let this be your guiding principle: When you tell a new international friend that you would like to get together, make sure you add that you would like to set up a time and place first.

9. *Show respect for superstitious beliefs.* Many cultures have an elaborate set of superstitions. Many are handed down from generation to generation, and children grow up believing them. Don't make fun of someone else's superstitions. Find out why they believe what they believe, and see if you can come up with a logical or scientific reason to gently counter it. If your friend gets agitated, drop the issue right away. And be prepared to defend your own beliefs, as some may counter your questions with questions of their own about Christianity.

10. *Keep in mind the distinctions between "high-context" and "low-context" cultures.* In some cultures the nonverbal aspect of communication plays a role that's as important as (or more important than) verbal communication. Gestures, posture, silence, and eye contact all play a significant role in communicating. These cultures are called "high-context" cultures. Cultures where the primary form of communication takes place through spoken words are called "low-context" cultures. You will need to be aware of this to better understand your international friend. Most Asian, African, and Latin American countries are high-context cultures, whereas low-context cultures can be found among Europeans, North Americans, Australians, and New Zealanders.

11. *Show respect for scriptures and places of worship.* In many cultures Scriptures and places of worship are considered holy and revered. If you treat the Bible disrespectfully, you are sure to alienate many of your international friends. Never let your feet touch the Bible. Never throw it around or fling it about. Also, if your church allows casual clothing and whistling and clapping during services, be prepared to explain why. This would be a highly uncomfortable surrounding for most internationals, especially those from Asia and Latin America.

12. *Show respect for other cultures and countries.* If you were in a foreign country and someone tried witnessing to you about another religion and then made fun of the United States, how effective would this person's witness be to you?

Not very. Keep this in mind if you're ever tempted to crack a joke about your new friend's culture or home country.

13. *Keep in mind the distinctions between collectivist and individualistic societies.* A collectivist society is one in which people tend to be part of a larger group, such as a family (including extended family), and the group is considered more important than the individual. The individual is loyal to the group and the group is loyal to the individual. In an individualistic society, the individual is responsible for himself and his immediate family only; the individual's values and decisions are not strongly influenced by the group. Most Western nations are individualistic societies, whereas most Asian, Latin American, and African countries are collectivist societies.

It is important to remember the distinction between the two. When you witness to a person from a collectivist society, he or she may seem persuaded but then refuse to make a decision. This happens because the person is acutely concerned about what his or her family may think. If the family is opposed to this person becoming a Christian, it could mean that he or she will be disowned by the family. A person from an individualistic society will probably not face such an agonizing situation. That is why it is important to build a relationship over a period of time with people from collectivist societies even as you witness to them. Also, introduce them to other members from their culture who are Christians (if you know of any).

Keep in mind that just because a person comes from a collectivist society doesn't mean he or she will be collectivist in nature, although most people are. Western influences have made strong inroads among the younger generation of many collectivist nations, and this has led to a tendency among the young to be more individualistic than collectivist.

14. *Show respect for the elderly.* In many cultures (especially collectivist societies), there is great respect for the elderly. Parents and grandparents are shown the utmost respect and honor. In many cases an individual cannot make an important decision unless the older members of the family approve it. When people from these cultures come to the United States, they are often shocked at the way older people are treated here. Showing disrespect to the elderly, sending

older members of the family to nursing homes, and openly disagreeing with them are often seen as brutal and cruel acts. Be prepared to discuss these issues if they ever come up.

15. *Be aware of the importance of saving face.* In many high-context cultures, it is important for people to save face or avoid feeling shame. In fact, in many of these cultures, one of the biggest insults you can inflict on someone is to say he or she is without shame or that he or she is shameless. For this reason, you should avoid criticizing someone in front of others. Although direct and candid conversation is appreciated by most of the low-context cultures (Western European and North American countries, Australia, and New Zealand), it can be perceived as highly offensive among people from high-context cultures (most Asian, African, and Latin American countries). In many of these cultures, open disagreement with someone is seen as insulting. In such cases, focus on similarities and start your conversation from common ground.

16. *Understand what it means to hold hands with someone of the same sex.* In many cultures it is common to find a man holding hands with another man. This doesn't necessarily have any sexual connotation; close friends of the same gender routinely hold hands. This practice is also common among women. So don't jump to conclusions. Furthermore, you may find that once your international friend (of the same sex as you) gets to know you, he or she might reach out and hold your hand. This is a sign of friendship—nothing more. If you feel uncomfortable, explain gently why this is viewed differently in America.

17. *Recognize the role of silence in conversation.* Among many Latin American, African, and Asian cultures, people have significant pauses in the midst of dialogue. For instance, you may say something, and your international friend will wait several seconds before replying. Don't rush to fill the silence. The silence signifies that your friend is showing respect for your opinion by thinking about it. This also indicates that your friend is thinking about his or her response.

18. *Be sensitive to customs regarding dating and marriage.* Many cultures have elaborate rules about dating and marriage. These rules are as varied as the cultures. People who were born in the United States are more assimilated into American culture, but many internationals view America as both promiscuous

and Christian. Unfortunately, they sometimes tie the two together. In many cultures a person can be disowned by his or her family and friends after marrying someone outside his or her culture. Some Hispanic cultures consider it highly inappropriate for a single woman to be alone with a man. In some Muslim circles a woman is likely to be looked down upon if she has a lot of male friends; this is especially true after marriage. Therefore, be very careful when interacting with someone of the opposite sex of another culture. If at all possible, interact with an opposite-sex person in a group setting.

19. *Be aware of how men from more traditional cultures may view women.* In many cultures, particularly those that are more traditional, women's roles are defined differently than here in the United States, as are expectations regarding how women should dress and how they should interact with men. For example, women in traditional cultures may not be allowed to teach or to hold a position of leadership (authority) over men. Women also may be expected to dress much more modestly than in America. (Shorts and short-sleeved tops are considered very immodest in some countries.) In some cultures, women do not make eye contact with men or shake hands.

While most international men living in America are accustomed to the way women here dress and to their leadership roles over men, some men from more traditional cultures may be shocked or offended by these differences. If you are an American woman, be aware of these potential differences and, if possible, avoid causing offense when you interact with men from traditional cultures. Above all, remember to show the love of Christ even if a man happens to respond negatively to you.

20. *Remember to smile!* The language of a smile (and conversely, a frown) is understood in every culture of the world. Smile! Remember, Christians have something to smile about.

21. *Be aware of other customs.* In many cultures people remove their shoes before entering a home. You may want to ask whether you should remove your shoes or not.

When giving gifts, keep in mind that certain gifts (such as clocks, knives, and umbrellas) have negative connotations in some cultures. On the other hand, red roses are almost universally considered to have romantic implications. Furthermore, in many cultures it is considered rude to open a gift in front of the giver.

Of course, no one can remember all the rules. When in doubt, ask. If your international friend offends *you* in any way, gently explain the offense. Only through clear and open communication can we discover the rich cultural mosaic that makes America such a great nation. And it will take us a step closer to forming friendships with our international neighbors.

Keep in mind the words of my pastor's wife, Sallie Fredericks, who is the evangelism director of our church: "People come to Christ best on the arm of a friend."

———

Part 2 of *Reaching the World in Our Own Backyard* is much like a road map. No one would ever be expected to remember all the roads and highways, cities, scenic routes, or other points of interest on a map. But it's a handy reference in times of need. Likewise, the following chapters are meant to serve as a handy reference guide that will help you better interact with people from other cultures. You may not be able to remember all of the information presented here, but you can refer back to it anytime you need help.

# 6

# Eastern Europe

This chapter provides specific information to help you relate to friends and acquaintances from Eastern European countries. For guidelines on interacting with internationals, please review the preceding chapter, "General Guidelines for Cross-Cultural Interaction."

## CZECH REPUBLIC

*Population:* 10.2 million

*Ethnicity:* Czech (94 percent), Slovak (3 percent), Other (3 percent)

*Religions/Religious Groups:* Atheist (40 percent), Roman Catholic (39 percent), Protestant (5 percent), Orthodox (3 percent), Other (13 percent)

*Language:* Czech

### How to Greet a Czech

- Use titles (such as Dr., Professor, Mr., Mrs., and so on) along with the last name of the person. Friends use first names.
- Handshakes are common, although men should wait for a woman to offer her hand first.

### Speak Czech!

A strong and immediate bridge can be built with your Czech friend if you know just a few phrases in his or her language. The fact that you took the trouble and made an attempt will mean a lot. You will develop rapport almost immediately and, invariably, evoke a smile. Here are some common phrases in Czech:

Hello: *Nazdar* (nahz-dar)

Good-bye: *Na shledanou* (nah shlay-da-no)

Good morning: *Dobre rano* (dob-ray rah-no)

Good afternoon: *Dobre odpoledne* (dob-ray ot-po-led-nay)

Good evening: *Dobry vecer* (dob-ree vay-cher)

Good night: *Dobrou noc* (dob-row nots)

How are you? *Jak se mas?* (yak say maash?)

Fine: *Dobre* (dob-ray)

Please: *Prosim* (pro-seem)

Thank you: *Dekuji* (dye-ku-yi)

Yes: *Jo* (yo)

No: *Ne* (nay)

### *Things to Remember When Interacting with a Czech*

- Czech culture is highly individualistic, which means your Czech friend is free to make a decision about the gospel without a lot of pressure from family members.
- In the past, religious expressions were suppressed by communism. Even today most Czechs are Atheists. Those who follow a religion are mostly nominal in their faith. Be prepared to present the gospel intellectually.
- Czechs may appear shy and reserved at first, but once you get to know them, most Czechs are friendly.
- If you are invited to a Czech home, it is customary to bring chocolates or unwrapped flowers—although you should bring only odd numbers of flowers (except one or thirteen). Avoid red roses because of their romantic implications, and lilies, which are associated with funerals.
- Czechs love sports—this is a safe topic for discussion.
- Czechs also love talking about their cultural heritage, especially music and literature.

- Some Czechs may ask personal questions. Be prepared to answer accordingly.
- If inviting or bringing a Czech friend to church, be prepared to explain any clapping or applause that may happen. Czechs don't applaud at church services.
- Pork roast and sauerkraut are among popular Czech meals.

### Be Aware of These Gestures

- Personal space among Czechs is smaller than in the United States, so don't be surprised if your Czech friend stands closer than you're accustomed to. Backing away is usually a mistake, as your Czech friend will simply step forward to close the gap.
- If invited to a Czech home, ask whether you should remove your shoes before entering the house.
- Don't keep your left hand in your pocket while shaking hands with your right hand.
- Don't put your hands in your pockets while talking.
- Chewing gum while talking is seen as rude.
- Maintain eye contact, but don't stare.

### Sensitive Issues

- Stay clear of Czech politics, especially relations with Slovakia.
- Avoid discussing communism and the former Soviet Union.
- Don't confuse Czechs with Germans.

## HUNGARY

*Population:* 10.1 million

*Ethnicity:* Hungarian (90 percent), Gypsy (4 percent), German (3 percent), Other (3 percent)

*Religions/Religious Groups:* Roman Catholic (68 percent), Calvinist (20 percent), Lutheran (5 percent), Other (7 percent)

*Language:* Hungarian

## How to Greet a Hungarian

- Use titles (such as Dr., Professor, Mr., Mrs., and so on) along with the last name of the person. Friends use first names.
- Handshakes are common, although men should wait for a woman to offer her hand first.

## Speak Hungarian!

A strong and immediate bridge can be built with your Hungarian friend if you know just a few phrases of the language. The fact that you took the trouble and made an attempt will mean a lot. You will develop rapport almost immediately and, invariably, evoke a smile. Here are some common phrases in Hungarian:

Hello: *Szia* (see-o)

Good-bye: *Viszontlatasra* (vee-son-tlay-taa-shro)

Good morning: *Jo reggelt* (yo ray-gaylt)

Good afternoon: *Jo napot* (yo nop-pot)

Good evening: *Jo estet* (yo es-tayt)

Good night: *Jo ejszakat* (yo ay-so-kaat)

How are you? *Hogy van?* (howd von?)

Fine: *Nagyon jol* (no-dawn yol)

Please: *Kerem* (kay-rem)

Thank you: *Koszonom* (koor-soor-nerm)

Yes: *Igen* (ee-gain)

No: *Nem* (name)

## Things to Remember When Interacting with a Hungarian

- Although Hungarian culture is becoming individualistic, most Hungarians will probably consider family members' opinions before making a final decision about the gospel. Chances are you may not get an immediate response, so be patient and support your Hungarian friend if he or she struggles spiritually.
- If you are invited to a Hungarian home, it is customary to bring chocolates or wrapped flowers—although you should bring only odd numbers

of flowers (except one or thirteen). Avoid red roses or chrysanthemums because of the implications.

- Don't waste food or leave any on your plate.
- A Hungarian can become self-deprecating when complimented.
- Soccer is a popular sport and a safe topic for discussion. Horses and Hungarian food are other great topics for conversation.
- Hungarians also love to talk about their artists and composers (Franz Liszt and Béla Bartók are among the well-known Hungarian composers).

### Be Aware of These Gestures

- Personal space among Hungarians is larger than in the United States. When conversing, don't be surprised if your Hungarian friend stands farther away than you're accustomed to. Don't step forward to close the gap.
- If invited to a Hungarian home, ask whether you should remove your shoes before entering the house.
- The sign for "okay" or "all right" (using the thumb and forefinger to make a circle) is regarded as an indignity.
- When visiting a Hungarian home, keep your hands above the table and not on your lap. However, don't put your elbows on the table.
- Don't point your feet or shoes at your Hungarian friend.
- Pointing with the index finger is considered rude.
- Avoid using your left hand while eating.

### Sensitive Issues

- Politics is a touchy topic that should be avoided.
- Avoid talking about Hungary's relations with its neighbors.

## POLAND

*Population:* 38.6 million
*Ethnicity:* Polish (98 percent), Other (2 percent)
*Religions/Religious Groups:* Roman Catholic (95 percent), Other (5 percent)
*Language:* Polish

*How to Greet a Pole*
- Use titles (such as Dr., Professor, Mr., Mrs., and so on) along with the last name of the person. Friends use first names.
- Handshakes are common, although men should wait for a woman to offer her hand first. Women should be greeted first.

*Speak Polish!*
A strong and immediate bridge can be built with your Polish friend if you know just a few phrases in his or her language. The fact that you took the trouble and made an attempt will mean a lot. You will develop rapport almost immediately and, invariably, evoke a smile. Here are some common phrases in Polish:

Hello: *Dzien dobry* (jeen dob-ree)
Good-bye: *Do widzenia* (doh vee-zee-nia)
Good morning: *Dzien dobry* (jeen dob-ree)
Good afternoon: *Dzien dobry* (jeen dob-ree)
Please: *Prosze* (pro-she)
Thank you: *Dziekuje* (jeen-ku-yi)
Yes: *Tak* (tahk)
No: *Nie* (nye)

*Things to Remember When Interacting with a Pole*
- Although Polish culture is becoming individualistic, some Poles may consider family members' opinions before making any final decisions about the gospel. Chances are you may not receive an immediate response, so be patient and support your Polish friend if he or she struggles spiritually.
- Poles are often generous and outspoken people.
- Your Polish friend may ask you personal questions. Be prepared for them.
- If you are invited to a Polish home, it is customary to bring unwrapped flowers—although you should bring only odd numbers (except one or thirteen). Avoid red roses or chrysanthemums because of the implications.

- Poles love talking about their cultural history, family, and Polish travel and tourism.

### Be Aware of These Gestures

- Personal space among Polish people is larger than in the United States. When conversing, don't be surprised if your Polish friend stands farther away than you're accustomed to. Don't step forward to close the gap.
- If a Pole touches his or her nose with the index finger, it means what has just been said is a joke and not really true.
- Giving a hug is rare.
- Chewing gum, especially at church, is regarded as impolite.
- When visiting a Polish home, keep your hands above the table and not on your lap. However, don't put your elbows on the table.
- Blinking both eyes at a woman denotes romantic implications.

### Sensitive Issues

- As in most other countries, politics is a sensitive issue—avoid the subject if you can.
- Avoid topics relating to World War II and past historic associations with Germany or the former Soviet Union.

## ROMANIA

*Population:* 22.3 million

*Ethnicity:* Romanian (89 percent), Hungarian (9 percent), Other (2 percent)

*Religions/Religious Groups:* Romanian Orthodox (70 percent), Roman Catholic (6 percent), Protestant (6 percent), Other (18 percent)

*Languages:* Romanian, Hungarian, and German

### How to Greet a Romanian

- Use titles (such as Dr., Professor, Mr., Mrs., and so on) along with the last name of the person. Friends use first names.

- Handshakes are common, although men should wait for a woman to offer her hand first.
- Men should stand when introduced to a woman.

### Speak Romanian!

A strong and immediate bridge can be built with your Romanian friend if you know just a few phrases in his or her language. The fact that you took the trouble and made an attempt will mean a lot to this person. You will develop rapport almost immediately and, invariably, evoke a smile. (Some Romanians also speak Hungarian and German. To learn the greetings in these languages, see the sections on Hungary and Germany.) Here are some common phrases in Romanian:

How do you do? *Ce mai faceti?* (chey mi-fachets?)

Good-bye: *La revedere* (lah ree-veh-deh-ray)

Good morning: *Buna dimineata* (boo-nuh dee-meen-yat-sah)

Good afternoon: *Buna ziua* (boo-nuh zee-wah)

Good evening: *Buna seara* (boo-nuh sia-rah)

Good night: *Noapte buna* (nwap-tay boo-nuh)

Please: *Va rog* (vah rohg)

Thank you: *Multumesc* (mool-too-mesk)

Yes: *Da* (dah)

No: *Nu* (noo)

### Things to Remember When Interacting with a Romanian

- Although Romanian culture is becoming individualistic, some Romanians may consider family members' opinions before making a final decision about the gospel. Chances are you may not get an immediate response, so be patient and support your Romanian friend if he or she struggles spiritually.
- If you are invited to a Romanian home, it is customary to bring wrapped flowers, although you should bring only odd numbers (except one or thirteen). Avoid red roses because of the romantic implications. Another good gift is coffee.

- Your Romanian friend may ask you personal questions. Be prepared for them.
- Romanians enjoy talking about books, sports, and travel.

### Be Aware of These Gestures
- Personal space among Romanians is smaller than in the United States. When conversing, don't be surprised if your Romanian friend stands closer than you're accustomed to. Backing away is usually a mistake, as your Romanian friend will simply step forward to close the gap.
- When visiting a Romanian home, keep your hands above the table and not on your lap. However, don't put your elbows on the table.
- Maintain eye contact, but don't stare.
- Don't put your hands in your pockets while talking.
- Chewing gum while talking is regarded as rude.

### Sensitive Issues
- Avoid discussing Romanian politics, especially the reign of Nicolae Ceauşescu.

## RUSSIA
*Population:* 145.5 million
*Ethnicity:* Russian (82 percent), Tartar (4 percent), Other (14 percent)
*Religions/Religious Groups:* Russian Orthodox, Muslim (no official statistics available)
*Language:* Russian

### How to Greet a Russian
- Use titles (such as Dr., Professor, Mr., Mrs., and so on) along with the last name of the person. Friends use first names.
- Handshakes are common, although men should wait for a woman to offer her hand first.

## Speak Russian!

A strong and immediate bridge can be built with your Russian friend if you know just a few phrases of the language. The fact that you took the trouble and made an attempt will mean a lot. You will develop rapport almost immediately and, invariably, evoke a smile. Here are some common phrases in Russian, which are written as they would be pronounced:

Hello: *Zdrast-voo-yet-yay*

Good-bye: *Dah-sui-dan-yah*

Good morning: *Dob-ray ut-rah*

Good afternoon: *Dob-ri dyen*

Good evening: *Dob-ri vye-cher*

Good night: *Spa-koi-nye no-chi*

How are you? *Kak vah-shi di-lah?*

Good or well: *Kah-rah-sho*

Please: *Paz-hal-us-tah*

Thank you: *Spa-see-bah*

Yes: *Dah*

No: *Nyet*

## Things to Remember When Interacting with a Russian

- Russian culture is collectivist. This means that most Russians will consider their acceptance of the gospel in the light of how it will impact their family and friends. Chances are you may not get an immediate response, so be patient and support your Russian friend if he or she struggles spiritually.
- If you are invited to a Russian home, it is customary to bring chocolates or flowers—but bring only odd numbers of flowers (except one or thirteen). Avoid red roses because of their romantic implications.
- After a meal, leave a little bit of food on your plate to signify that you are satisfied. If you don't, your host will think you are still hungry.
- Russians tend to be highly reserved in public. They are much more expressive in private among friends and family members.

- Since many Russians are from an Orthodox background, they find it hard to adjust to churches that allow informal attire. Be prepared to explain why people wear shorts, jeans, or otherwise casual attire in the house of God.
- Ballet is a safe and welcome topic of conversation. Other safe topics include art, theater, and sports.

## Be Aware of These Gestures

- Personal space among Russians is smaller than in the United States. When conversing, don't be surprised if your Russian friend stands closer than you're accustomed to. Backing away is usually a mistake, as your Russian friend will simply step forward to close the gap.
- If invited to a Russian home, ask whether you should remove your shoes before entering the house.
- The sign for "okay" or "all right" (using the thumb and forefinger to make a circle) is regarded as an indignity.
- The *V* for victory sign (extending just the index and middle fingers) is considered rude.
- Whistling in public is considered impolite. In fact, whistling can also be seen as a sign of disagreement. So if there is whistling at your church, be prepared to explain to your Russian friend why church members are "disagreeing" with the pastor or the speaker.
- When visiting a Russian home, keep your hands above the table and not on your lap. However, don't put your elbows on the table.
- Don't point your feet or shoes at your Russian friend.
- Pointing with the index finger is considered rude.
- Don't put your hands in your pockets while talking.
- Some Russians consider it bad luck to shake hands across the threshold of a home.

## Sensitive Issues

- Avoid initiating conversations on politics and communism.

# 7

# Western Europe

This chapter provides specific information to help you relate to friends and acquaintances from Western European countries. For guidelines on interacting with internationals, please review chapter 5, "General Guidelines for Cross-Cultural Interaction."

## Belgium

*Population:* 10.3 million

*Ethnicity:* Fleming (55 percent), Walloon (33 percent), Other (12 percent)

*Religions/Religious Groups:* Roman Catholic (75 percent), Other (25 percent)

*Languages:* Dutch, French, and German

### How to Greet a Belgian

- Use titles (such as Dr., Professor, Mr., Mrs., and so on) along with the last name of the person. Friends use first names.
- Handshakes are common, although men should wait for a woman to offer her hand first.
- To learn greetings in Dutch, French, and German, see the sections on the Netherlands, France, and Germany. Speaking to your Belgian friend in his or her language will help you create rapport.

*Things to Remember When Interacting with a Belgian*
- Belgian culture is highly individualistic, which means your Belgian friend is free to make his or her own decision about the gospel without a lot of pressure from family members.
- Keep in mind that most Belgians are ethnically divided into two groups: Dutch-speaking Flemish or French-speaking Walloon. Don't get into talking about their linguistic or cultural differences.
- Sports (especially soccer), art, and food are good and safe topics of conversation.
- Belgians are very proud of their cultural heritage, so steer the conversation to this area, and you will find your Belgian friend sharing a lot about this beautiful country.
- If you are invited to a Belgian home, it is customary to bring flowers— although you should bring only odd numbers (except one or thirteen). Avoid red roses or chrysanthemums because of their implications. Another good gift is chocolate.
- At meals with your Belgian friend, don't waste food or leave any on your plate.
- Favorite foods of Belgians include breads, soups, pork, and fish.

*Be Aware of These Gestures*
- Personal space among Belgians is larger than in the United States. When conversing, don't be surprised if your Belgian friend stands farther away than you may be accustomed to. Don't step forward to close the gap.
- Pointing with the index finger is considered rude.
- Snapping your fingers is considered impolite.
- Don't put your feet on a table or furniture.
- Avoid using toothpicks in public.
- Try not to yawn in front of your Belgian friend. If you have to yawn, cover your mouth when doing so.
- Chewing gum while talking is regarded as rude.

- Don't put your hands in your pockets while talking.
- When visiting a Belgian home, keep your hands above the table and not on your lap. However, don't put your elbows on the table.

### Sensitive Issues

- Avoid discussions on the distinctions between Dutch-speaking Flemish and French-speaking Walloons.
- Don't ask personal questions. Belgians tend to be very private people.

## FRANCE

*Population:* 59.6 million

*Ethnicity:* Celtic and Latin with several minorities such as Teutonic, Slavic, North African, Indochinese, and Basque

*Religions/Religious Groups:* Roman Catholic (90 percent), Other—including Muslims, Jews, and Protestants (10 percent)

*Language:* French

### How to Greet a French Person

- Use titles (such as Dr., Professor, Mr., Mrs., and so on) along with the last name of the person. Your French friend will soon encourage you to switch to a first-name basis.
- Handshakes are common, although men should wait for a woman to offer her hand first.

### Speak French!

A strong and immediate bridge can be built if you know just a few phrases of the French language. The fact that you took the trouble and made an attempt will mean a lot to your international friend. You will develop rapport almost immediately and, invariably, evoke a smile. Here are some common phrases in French:

Hello: *Bonjour* (bone-zure)

Nice to meet you: *Enchanté* (ahn-shahn-tay)

Good-bye: *Au revoir* (oh ray-vwah)

Good day: *Bonjour* (bone-zure)

Good evening: *Bonsoir* (bone-swar)

Good night: *Bonne nuit* (bone-newee)

How are you? *Comment allez-vous?* (kommon allay voo?)

Fine: *Ça va* (sah vah)

Please: *S'il vous plait* (seel voo play)

Thank you: *Merci* (mare-see)

Yes: *Oui* (wee)

No: *Non* (noh, with a nasal "oh")

### *Things to Remember When Interacting with a French Person*

- French culture is highly individualistic, which means your French friend is free to make his or her own decision about the gospel without a lot of pressure from family members.
- French people tend to be friendly and humorous.
- The French talk in a softer voice than Americans. Keep your volume on the same level.
- If you are invited to a French home, it is customary to bring candy, pastries, cookies, or flowers—although you should bring only odd numbers of flowers (except one or thirteen). Avoid red roses or chrysanthemums because of their implications. Also, wait to be told where to sit.
- French art, history, and sports are good topics of conversation.
- Most French people love a stimulating discussion. If you get into a discussion on religion with a French person, expect a rousing and vigorous debate. Be prepared to defend your faith intellectually, but don't be aggressive.
- Elderly French people are fond of their World War II American allies. This is a good topic for conversation among this group.

### *Be Aware of These Gestures*

- Personal space among French people is smaller than in the United States. When conversing with your French friend, don't be surprised if he or she stands closer than you're accustomed to. Backing away is usually a mistake, as your French friend will simply step forward to close the gap.

- When visiting a French home, keep your hands above the table and not on your lap. However, don't put your elbows on the table.
- Putting your feet on a table or on other furniture is considered rude.
- Don't put your hands in your pockets while talking.
- Avoid using toothpicks or combs in public.
- Pointing with the index finger is considered rude.
- Don't snap your fingers. It is considered impolite.
- Chewing gum while talking is regarded as rude.
- The sign for "okay" or "all right" (using the thumb and forefinger to make a circle) means "zero" or "worthless."

### Sensitive Issues
- Keep away from political discussions.
- Don't get into personal issues or questions.
- Stay away from discussions on money matters.

## GERMANY

*Population:* 83 million
*Ethnicity:* German (92 percent), Turkish (2 percent), Other (6 percent)
*Religions/Religious Groups:* Protestant (38 percent), Roman Catholic (34 percent), Other (28 percent)
*Language:* German

### How to Greet a German
- Use titles (such as Dr., Professor, Mr., Mrs., and so on) along with the last name of the person. Friends use first names.
- Handshakes are common, although men should wait for a woman to offer her hand first.

*Speak German!*

A strong and immediate bridge can be built if you know just a few phrases of the German language. The fact that you took the trouble and made an attempt will mean a lot to your German friend. You will develop rapport almost immediately and, invariably, evoke a smile. Here are some common phrases in German:

Good morning: *Guten morgen* (goo-ten mor-gen)

Good afternoon: *Guten tag* (goo-ten tahg)

Good night: *Guten abend* (goo-ten ah-burnt)

Good-bye: *Auf Wiedersehen* (off vee-der-zay-urn)

How are you? *Wie geht es ihnen?* (vee gait ehs inn-urn?)

Fine, thanks: *Danke, gut* (dahn-ker goot)

Please: *Bitte* (bit-ter)

Thank you: *Danke* (dahn-ker)

Yes: *Ja* (yaa)

No: *Nein* (nine)

*Things to Remember When Interacting with a German*

- German culture is highly individualistic, which means your German friend is free to make his or her own decision about the gospel without a lot of pressure from family members.
- Germans tend to be formal and polite and dislike any kind of loud behavior.
- If you are invited to a German home, it is customary to bring unwrapped flowers—although you should bring only odd numbers (except one or thirteen). Avoid red roses and lilies because of their implications. Also, carnations are associated with mourning.
- Don't waste food or leave any on your plate.
- Safe topics for conversation include hobbies, weather, travel, and sports (soccer is popular in Germany).
- Germans tend to be private people. Any attempt to build a personal relationship should be undertaken over a period of time.

- Although they tend to be private and formal, most Germans like to discuss religion. You may get a good opening to talk about the gospel, but be prepared to present it intellectually.
- If inviting a German for a meal, keep in mind that most Germans love meat, potatoes, and noodles.

### Be Aware of These Gestures

- Personal space among Germans is larger than in the United States. When conversing, don't be surprised if your German friend stands farther away than you're accustomed to. Don't step forward to close the gap.
- Don't keep your left hand in your pocket while shaking hands with your right hand.
- Don't put your hands in your pockets while talking.
- The sign for "okay" or "all right" (using the thumb and forefinger to make a circle) is regarded as an indignity.
- When visiting a German home, keep your hands above the table and not on your lap. However, don't put your elbows on the table.
- Don't put your feet on a table or on other furniture.
- Don't chew gum while talking.

### Sensitive Issues

- Keep away from political discussions.
- Don't get into personal issues or questions.
- Stay totally clear of any discussion about World War II, Nazis, skinheads, and so on.

## GREECE

*Population:* 10.6 million
*Ethnicity:* Greek (98 percent), Other (2 percent)
*Religions/Religious Groups:* Greek Orthodox (98 percent), Other (2 percent)
*Language:* Greek

## How to Greet a Greek

- Use titles (such as Dr., Professor, Mr., Mrs., and so on) along with the last name of the person. Friends use first names.
- Handshakes are common.

## Speak Greek!

A strong and immediate bridge can be built with your Greek friend if you know just a few phrases in his or her language. The fact that you took the trouble and made an attempt will mean a lot to your Greek friend. You will develop rapport almost immediately and, invariably, evoke a smile. Here are some common Greek phrases, which are written as they would be pronounced:

Good morning: *Kah-lee-may-rah*

Good afternoon: *Kah-lee-spay-rah*

Good night: *Kah-lee-nix-tah*

Good-bye: *Ahn-dee-o*

How are you? *Poss es-tay?*

Fine, thanks: *Paw-lee kah-lah*

Please: *Paa-raa-kah-lo*

Thank you: *eff-kah-rees-toh*

Yes: *Neh*

No: *O-kee*

## Things to Remember When Interacting with a Greek

- Greek culture is mostly collectivist. This means that most Greeks will consider their acceptance of the gospel in light of how it will impact their family and friends. Chances are you may not get an immediate response, so be patient and support your Greek friend if he or she struggles spiritually.
- A common custom that may surprise you is the asking of personal questions. Be prepared for them.
- Safe topics of conversation include sports, Greek history, and culture.

- When sharing the gospel, you may find that your Greek friend becomes vivacious in the discussion. This is a good sign! Don't back down. It is normal for Greeks to be lively in discussions when they are interested. Of course, if you feel your Greek friend is getting annoyed and irritated, switch subjects.
- When you are invited to a Greek home, it is customary to bring cake, cookies, or flowers. Avoid red roses because of their romantic implications.
- Greeks are highly generous people. Be careful not to praise an object too much, or it may be given to you!
- After a meal, don't leave any food on your plate. This will signify that you are satisfied. Don't get up from the table until your host does.
- Greeks have great respect for the elderly.
- Favorite foods include lamb, chicken, cheese, olives, and potatoes.

### Be Aware of These Gestures
- The sign for "okay" or "all right" (using the thumb and forefinger to make a circle) is regarded as an affront.
- Sometimes a Greek may shake his or her head side to side to indicate understanding or affirmation—or up and down to indicate a negative response (exactly the opposite of how these gestures are viewed in America).
- When visiting a Greek home, keep your hands above the table and not on your lap. However, don't put your elbows on the table.
- Pointing with the index finger is considered rude.

### Sensitive Issues
- As in most other countries, avoid talking about Greek politics.
- Don't raise the topic of Cyprus or Turkey with a Greek.
- Never criticize your Greek friend in front of others. It will be considered highly offensive.

## IRELAND

*Population:* 3.8 million

*Ethnicity:* Celtic, English (no official statistics available)

*Religions/Religious Groups:* Roman Catholic (93 percent), Anglican (3 percent), Other (4 percent)

*Languages:* English and Irish (Gaelic)

### How to Greet an Irish Person

- Use titles (such as Dr., Professor, Mr., Mrs., and so on) along with the last name of the person. Friends use first names.
- Handshakes are common.

### Things to Remember When Interacting with an Irish Person

- Although Irish culture is somewhat individualistic, most Irish people will probably consider family members' opinions before making any final decisions about the gospel. Chances are you may not get an immediate response, so be prepared to support your Irish friend if he or she struggles spiritually.
- Irish people are friendly and outgoing. However, religion is an uncomfortable topic. Be creative in approaching it. Any situation, problem, or event could be an opportunity, but be sensitive.
- Some good topics for conversation are Irish culture, dance, sports, and Irish heritage in the United States.
- Don't waste food or leave any on your plate.
- If you are invited to an Irish home, it is customary to bring chocolates or flowers. Avoid red roses because of their romantic implications.

### Be Aware of These Gestures

- Personal space among Irish people is larger than in the United States. When conversing with your Irish friend, don't be surprised if he or she stands farther away than you are accustomed to. Don't step forward to close the gap.

- Avoid physical contact of any kind (other than handshakes). Irish people don't like physical contact with strangers.
- The *V* for victory sign (extending just the index and middle fingers with the palm facing outward) is considered an obscene gesture.
- Don't comb your hair in front of your Irish friend.

### Sensitive Issues
- As in most other countries, politics is a sensitive issue—avoid this topic.
- Your Irish friend may criticize Irish politics and life, but you shouldn't join in. Do more listening than talking.
- Don't talk about the island of Ireland being divided into two nations. (Northern Ireland is part of the United Kingdom.)
- Don't confuse Ireland with Great Britain.
- Don't criticize your Irish friend in front of others.
- Irish people don't like confrontations.

## ITALY
*Population:* 57.7 million
*Ethnicity:* Italian
*Religions/Religious Groups:* Predominantly Roman Catholic (98 percent)
*Languages:* Italian, German, and French

### How to Greet an Italian
- Use titles (such as Dr., Professor, Mr., Mrs., and so on) along with the last name of the person. Friends use first names.
- Handshakes are common, although men should wait for a woman to offer her hand first.

### Speak Italian!
A strong and immediate bridge can be built if you know just a few phrases of the Italian language. The fact that you took the trouble and made an attempt will mean a lot to your international friend. You will develop rapport almost

immediately and, invariably, evoke a smile. Here are some common phrases in Italian (some Italians speak German and French—look under Germany and France to learn a few phrases in those languages):

Hello: *Ciao* (chow)

Good morning: *Buon giorno* (bwon jo-ar-noah)

Good afternoon: *Buon giorno* (bwon jo-ar-noah)

Good night: *Buona notte* (bwo-nah not-tay)

Good-bye: *Arrivederci* (ah-ree-vay-dare-chee)

How are you? *Come sta?* (ko-may stah?)

Fine, thanks: *Bene grazie* (bay-nay graht-see-ay)

Please: *Per favore* (payr fah-vo-ray)

Thank you: *Grazie* (graht-see-ay)

Yes: *Si* (see)

No: *No* (noh)

### *Things to Remember When Interacting with an Italian*

- Although Italian culture is somewhat individualistic, some Italians will probably consider family members' opinions before making any final decisions about the gospel. Chances are you may not get an immediate response, so be patient and support your Italian friend if he or she struggles spiritually.
- Safe topics of conversation include news, international events, Italian food, and soccer. Some Italians may even dwell on family matters.
- If invited to an Italian home, it is customary to bring chocolates or flowers—but bring only odd numbers of flowers (except one or thirteen). Avoid red roses or chrysanthemums because of their implications.
- When invited to an Italian home, wait until everyone is served before beginning to eat. Also, keep in mind that lunches during holidays or special occasions can be several hours long. Don't be surprised if you are constantly interrupted while talking. This is considered normal.
- Expect conversations with your Italian friend to be lively. Most Italians are very expressive.

## Be Aware of These Gestures

- Personal space among Italians is smaller than in the United States. When conversing, don't be surprised if your Italian friend stands closer than you're accustomed to. Backing away is usually a mistake, as your Italian friend will simply step forward to close the gap.
- The sign for "okay" or "all right" (using the thumb and forefinger to make a circle) is viewed as an indignity.
- Maintain eye contact, but don't stare.
- Italians are arguably the most gesticulating people in the world. Expect a plethora of hand and head gestures while conversing with an Italian.
- Cover your mouth when yawning.
- Don't remove your shoes in front of your Italian friend.
- When visiting an Italian home, keep your hands above the table and not on your lap. However, don't put your elbows on the table.
- Don't use your hands to pick up cheese—use a fork instead.

## Sensitive Issues

- As in most other countries, politics is a sensitive issue—avoid talking about it. Also, stay clear of initiating discussions on World War II.
- Some Italians don't like being asked about their profession.
- Avoid talking about the Mafia.

## THE NETHERLANDS

*Population:* 16 million

*Ethnicity:* Dutch (94 percent), Other—including Moroccans and Turks (6 percent)

*Religions/Religious Groups:* Roman Catholic (34 percent), Protestant (25 percent), Other (41 percent)

*Language:* Dutch

## How to Greet a Dutch Person

- Use titles, although your Dutch friend will probably encourage you to use his or her first name. Dutch people are relaxed and easygoing.

- Handshakes are common. Make sure you shake hands with men, women, and children. Women might take it as an insult if you shake hands with men and avoid them.

## Speak Dutch!

A strong and immediate bridge can be built with your Dutch friend if you know just a few phrases of his or her language. The fact that you took the trouble and made an attempt will mean a lot to your international friend. You will develop rapport almost immediately and, invariably, evoke a smile. Here are some common phrases in Dutch:

Hello: *Hallo* (hullo)

Good-bye: *Tot ziens* (tot zeens)

Good morning: *Goede morgen* (hoo-der mor-hen)

Good afternoon: *Goede middag* (hoo-der mid-duck)

Please: *Alstublieft* (uls-too-bleeft)

Thank you: *Dank u* (dunk oo)

Yes: *Ja* (yah)

No: *Nee* (nay)

## Things to Remember When Interacting with a Dutch Person

- Dutch culture is highly individualistic, which means your Dutch friend is free to make his or her own decision about the gospel without a lot of pressure from family members.
- The Dutch love talking about their famous artists (which include Rembrandt and Van Gogh), music, and international affairs.
- As in most other European countries, sports is a safe topic. Soccer is a very popular sport in Holland.
- If you are invited to a Dutch home, it is customary to bring chocolates or unwrapped flowers. Avoid red roses because of their romantic implications. Also, men should wait until ladies are seated before taking their seats.
- My wife and I visited a Dutch restaurant in Orlando and were surprised at the variety of seafood Dutch people eat. Fish and potatoes are among their favorite foods.

## *Be Aware of These Gestures*

- Personal space among the Dutch people is larger than in the United States. When conversing, don't be surprised if your Dutch friend stands farther away than you're accustomed to. Don't step forward to close the gap.
- Avoid physical contact of any kind (other than handshakes). Dutch people don't like physical contact with strangers.
- Don't keep your left hand in your pocket while shaking hands with your right hand.
- When visiting a Dutch home, keep your hands above the table and not on your lap. However, don't put your elbows on the table.
- Eat all the food you take. Leaving food on your plate may be seen as a sign that you did not enjoy the meal. Also, once you start, don't get up until you have finished eating (plan ahead—use the bathroom before you start eating).
- Maintain eye contact, but don't stare.
- Cover your mouth when yawning.
- Don't put your hands in your pockets while talking.
- Chewing gum while talking is regarded as impolite.

## *Sensitive Issues*

- The Dutch are sensitive about religion and personal beliefs. Unless you feel compelled by the Spirit, wait until you get to know your Dutch friend better before broaching the topic.
- Don't make fun of or otherwise belittle Dutch royalty. They are highly regarded by most Dutch people.
- Don't ask personal questions. The Dutch tend to be very private people.
- As is the case with people from most other countries, avoid discussions about politics.

## NORWAY

*Population:* 4.5 million

*Ethnicity:* Norwegian

*Religions/Religious Groups:* Officially Evangelical Lutheran (88 percent), Other
    (12 percent)
*Language:* Norwegian

### How to Greet a Norwegian

- Use titles (such as Dr., Professor, Mr., Mrs., and so on) along with the
  last name of the person. Friends use first names.
- Handshakes are common.

### Speak Norwegian!

A strong and immediate bridge can be built with your Norwegian friend if you
know just a few phrases in his or her language. The fact that you took the trouble
and made an attempt will mean a lot to your friend. You will develop rapport
almost immediately and, invariably, evoke a smile. Here are some common
phrases in Norwegian:

Good morning: *God morgen* (goo maw-urn)
Good day: *God dag* (goo dahg)
Good night: *God natt* (goo naht)
Good-bye: *Adjo* (ad-your)
How are you? *Hvordan star det til?* (voo-dahn staur day till?)
Fine, thanks: *Bare bra, takk* (bahrer brah tahk)
Thank you: *Takk* (tahk)
Yes: *Ja* (yah)
No: *Nei* (nay)

### Things to Remember When Interacting with a Norwegian

- Norwegian culture is highly individualistic, which means your Norwe-
  gian friend is free to make his or her own decision about the gospel
  without a lot of pressure from family members.
- Norwegians tend to talk in a low voice and dislike loud behavior.
- Norwegian history, culture, and travel are safe discussion topics.
- Sports and hobbies are safe topics for conversation.
- Most Norwegians are strong environmentalists.

- If you are invited to a Norwegian home, it is customary to bring chocolates or flowers. Avoid red roses because of their romantic implications. Also avoid lilies, carnations, and white flowers, as they are associated with funerals.
- If invited to dine at a Norwegian friend's house, keep in mind that Norwegian meals tend to have several courses and can last a long time. Try not to waste food or leave anything on your plate.

### *Be Aware of These Gestures*

- Personal space among Norwegians is larger than in the United States. When conversing, don't be surprised if your Norwegian friend stands farther away than you are accustomed to. Don't step forward to close the gap.
- When visiting a Norwegian home, keep your hands above the table and not on your lap. However, don't put your elbows on the table.
- Don't put your hands in your pockets while talking.
- Cover your mouth when yawning.
- Chewing gum while talking is seen as rude.
- The sign for "okay" or "all right" (extending just the thumb and forefinger to make a circle) is regarded as an insult.

### *Sensitive Issues*

- Norwegians don't like being compared to other Scandinavian countries. They feel Americans sometimes don't see them as a separate culture from the Swedish or Danish cultures.
- Avoid personal questions. Most Norwegians are very private people.
- Avoid comparing the United States with Norway.

## SPAIN

*Population:* 40 million
*Ethnicity:* Combination of Mediterranean and Nordic backgrounds
*Religions/Religious Groups:* Roman Catholic (99 percent), Other (1 percent)
*Language:* Spanish

## *How to Greet a Spaniard*

- When appropriate, use titles (such as Dr., Professor, and so on) along with the last name of the person. Refer to nonprofessionals as Señor (Mr.), Señora (Mrs.), or Señorita (Miss) followed by their last name. Friends use first names.

- Handshakes are common, although men should wait for a woman to offer her hand first.

## *Speak Spanish!*

A strong and immediate bridge can be built if you know just a few phrases of Spanish. The fact that you took the trouble and made an attempt will mean a lot to your Spanish friend. You will develop rapport almost immediately and, invariably, evoke a smile. Here are some common phrases in Spanish:

Hello: *Hola* (oh-lah)

Good-bye: *Hasta luego* (ahs-tah lwey-go)

Good morning/Good day: *Buenos días* (bwey-nohs dee-ahs)

Good evening: *Buenas tardes* (bwe-nahs tar-dehs)

Good night: *Buenas noches* (bwe-nahs know-chess)

How are you? *¿Cómo está usted?* (koh-moh es-tah oos-tehd?)

Very well, thank you: *Muy bien, gracias* (moo-ee bien grah-see-ehs)

Please: *Por favor* (por fah-vor)

Thank you: *Gracias* (grah-see-ehs)

Yes: *Sí* (see)

No: *No* (no)

## *Things to Remember When Interacting with a Spaniard*

- Although Spanish culture is somewhat individualistic, most Spaniards will probably consider family members' opinions before making any final decisions about the gospel. Chances are you may not get an immediate response, so be patient and support your Spanish friend if he or she struggles spiritually.

- Safe topics of conversation include families, Spanish history, and culture.

- Another good topic of conversation is sports—soccer or *fútbol* (pronounced foot-bole) is a favorite of most Spaniards.
- If you are invited to a Spanish home, it is customary to bring chocolates or flowers. Avoid red roses because of their romantic implications. Also avoid chrysanthemums and dahlias.
- Don't waste food or leave any on your plate.
- Don't be surprised if you are constantly interrupted while talking. This is considered normal.
- Expect conversations with your Spanish friend to be lively. Spaniards are very expressive.
- Don't be surprised (or take offense) if your Spanish friend gives you advice on different issues. This is considered acceptable and is even expected in Spain. Just be careful about giving advice in return.

### Be Aware of These Gestures

- Personal space among Spanish people is smaller than in the United States. When conversing, don't be surprised if your Spanish friend stands closer than you're accustomed to. Backing away is usually a mistake, as your Spanish friend will simply step forward to close the gap.
- Sometimes a Spaniard may shake his or her head from side to side to indicate understanding or affirmation (or a yes)—or up and down to indicate a no (exactly the opposite of how these gestures are viewed here in America).
- The sign for "okay" or "all right" (extending just the thumb and forefinger to make a circle) is regarded as an indignity.
- When visiting a Spanish home, keep your hands above the table and not on your lap. However, don't put your elbows on the table.
- Pointing with the index finger is considered rude.
- Chewing gum while talking is regarded as rude.
- Try not to yawn in front of your Spanish friend. If you have to yawn, cover your mouth. Yawning in public is considered rude behavior.

- Don't keep your hands in your pockets while talking.

*Sensitive Issues*
- One mistake American Christians (especially those who feel strongly about animal rights) make when interacting with Spaniards is to be critical of bullfighting. To a Spaniard, bullfighting is a sport. Criticizing bullfighting would be tantamount to criticizing Spanish culture.
- Don't compare Spain to the United States, since Spain is one of the poorest countries in Western Europe.
- Although your Spanish friend may seem interested in talking about politics, you should concentrate on listening rather than talking.
- Don't criticize your Spanish friend in front of others. Personal honor is very important to a Spaniard.

## SWEDEN
*Population:* 8.9 million
*Ethnicity:* Homogeneous Caucasian population with a significant immigrant minority
*Religions/Religious Groups:* Evangelical Lutheran (94 percent), Other (6 percent)
*Language:* Swedish

*How to Greet a Swede*
- Use titles (such as Dr., Professor, Mr., Mrs., and so on) along with the last name of the person. Friends go by first names.
- Handshakes are common.
- A common form of greeting is *God dag* (pronounced goo dahg), which means "Good Day."

*Speak Swedish!*
A strong and immediate bridge can be built with your Swedish friend if you know just a few phrases in his or her language. The fact that you took the trouble and made an attempt will mean a lot. You will develop rapport almost

immediately and, invariably, evoke a smile. Here are some common phrases in Swedish:

Hello: *Hej* (hey)

Good-bye: *Adjo* (ay-your)

Good morning: *God morgen* (goo more-on)

Good afternoon: *God middag* (goo mid-dahg)

Good evening: *God afton* (goo aff-ton)

Good night: *God natt* (goo nut)

How are you? *Hur star det till?* (hure staur date till?)

Fine, thanks: *Bra, tack* (brah, tahk)

Please: *Tack* (tahk)

Thank you: *Tack* (tahk)

Yes: *Ja* (yah)

No: *Nej* (nay)

### *Things to Remember When Interacting with a Swede*

- Swedish culture is highly individualistic, which means your Swedish friend is free to make his or her own decision about the gospel without a lot of pressure from family members.
- Swedes tend to talk in a low voice and dislike loud behavior.
- Swedes tend to be highly reserved.
- Swedes love talking about sports and movies. Soccer is a popular sport. Swedes also love skiing.
- Sweden is the birthplace of the Nobel Prize.
- If you are invited to a Swedish home, it is customary to bring cake, chocolates, or flowers—although you should bring only odd numbers of flowers (except one or thirteen). Avoid red roses because of their romantic implications.
- Don't waste food or leave any on your plate, as this is considered rude. After the meal, make sure you thank your host *before* getting up from the table.
- You may find your Swedish friend to be practical and direct. Be prepared to share the gospel intellectually.

## Be Aware of These Gestures

- Personal space among Swedes is larger than in the United States. When conversing, don't be surprised if your Swedish friend stands farther away than you're accustomed to. Don't step forward to close the gap.
- If invited to a Swedish home, ask whether you should remove your shoes before entering the house. This is a common practice in Sweden.
- Swedes are friendly but do not use a lot of gestures. Be careful about gesturing too much.
- When visiting a Swedish home, keep your hands above the table and not on your lap. However, don't put your elbows on the table.
- Don't keep your hands in your pockets while talking.
- Try not to yawn in front of your Swedish friend. If you have to yawn, cover your mouth.
- Chewing gum while talking is regarded as rude.
- Maintain eye contact, but don't stare.

## Sensitive Issues

- As is the case with most other countries, avoid discussing politics. Don't criticize the Swedish government or culture even if your Swedish friend does.
- Don't get into personal issues or questions. Wait until you get to know your Swedish friend a little better.
- Don't confuse Swedish culture with Scandinavian culture, which includes other Scandinavian countries.
- The indigenous people of Sweden should be called *Sami,* not *Lapps,* which is considered a derogatory term.

## SWITZERLAND

*Population:* 7.3 million

*Ethnicity:* German (65 percent), French (18 percent), Italian (10 percent), Other (7 percent)

*Religions/Religious Groups:* Roman Catholic (46 percent), Protestant (40 percent), Other (14 percent)

*Languages:* German, French, and Italian

### How to Greet a Swiss Person

- Use titles (such as Dr., Professor, Mr., Mrs., and so on) along with the last name of the person. Friends use first names.
- Shake hands with everyone present, including children.
- To learn a few phrases in the languages spoken in Switzerland, see the sections on Germany, France, and Italy. This will help create an immediate rapport with your Swiss friend.

### Things to Remember When Interacting with a Swiss Person

- Swiss culture is individualistic, which means your Swiss friend is free to make his or her own decision about the gospel without a lot of pressure from family members.
- Swiss people tend to be reserved.
- Safe topics of conversation include current world affairs, Switzerland's natural beauty, and sports. Soccer is a popular sport. The Swiss also love hiking.
- Keep in mind that Switzerland has one of the world's highest standards of living and per capita income. However, the Swiss still tend to be conservative. Some people consider the Swiss to be impersonal. Be prepared to share the gospel intellectually.
- Switzerland, in one sense, is a multicultural society with people of German, Italian, and French heritage.
- If you are invited to a Swiss home, it is customary to bring chocolates or unwrapped flowers—although you should bring only odd numbers of flowers (except one or thirteen). Avoid red roses because of their romantic implications.
- Don't waste food or leave any on your plate. This may offend your Swiss host.

## *Be Aware of These Gestures*

- When visiting a Swiss home, keep your hands above the table and not on your lap. However, don't put your elbows on the table.
- Pointing with the index finger is considered an obscene gesture.
- Don't put your hands in your pockets while talking.
- Chewing gum while talking is regarded as rude.

## *Sensitive Issues*

- Like the Spaniards, the Swiss love talking about politics. Again, you should do more listening than talking.
- Avoid personal questions.

## UNITED KINGDOM

*Population:* 59.6 million

*Ethnicity:* English (82 percent), Scottish (10 percent), Irish (2 percent), Other (6 percent)

*Religions/Religious Groups:* Anglican (45 percent), Other—including Protestant, Muslim, and Hindu (40 percent), Roman Catholic (15 percent)

*Languages:* English and Welsh

## *How to Greet a Briton*

- Use titles (such as Dr., Professor, Mr., Mrs., and so on) along with the last name of the person. Friends use first names.
- Handshakes are common.
- Britons prefer to use "Hello" when greeting and add "How are you?" if the person they are greeting is known to them.

## *Things to Remember When Interacting with a Briton*

- The United Kingdom includes England, Scotland, Wales, and Northern Ireland. If you leave out Northern Ireland, the other three are collectively known as Great Britain.

- Briton culture is highly individualistic, which means your friend is free to make his or her own decision about the gospel without a lot of pressure from family members.
- One estimate says only about 10 percent of all adults in the United Kingdom attend church regularly. Many feel they don't need God. Be prepared to present the gospel intellectually.
- Although many Americans think of Britons as reserved and polite, they are often friendly once you get to know them.
- Use "Please" and "Thank you" where appropriate—Britons are incredibly sensitive to manners.
- An easy way to start a conversation with a Briton is by discussing the weather.
- Britons will not always say what they think, so use open-ended questions (such as "What do you think about that?") in your conversations.
- Although initially shy, a Briton will open up and discuss his or her innermost thoughts once trust is established.
- Most elderly people from the United Kingdom long for company, so they will appreciate your attention.
- Britons are often suspicious of strangers, so keep the opening fairly neutral and your approach reserved.
- Britons might be intimidated by the noise and passion of a contemporary church. If your church falls into this category, start by inviting your friend to nonthreatening events such as plays, concerts, picnics, and so on.
- Safe topics of conversation are U.K. cultural history and sports. Football (or soccer) is a popular sport. Britons also love cricket and tennis.
- Britons love beef and vegetables. However, due to health scares in recent years, a growing number have turned to seafood, curries, and vegetarian dishes.
- Keep in mind that many English words mean different things in the United Kingdom and America (ask your friend if in doubt). For

instance, an *elevator* is called a *lift,* *French fries* are called *chips,* and a *flashlight* is called a *torch.*

- If you are invited to the home of a Briton, bring chocolates or flowers. Avoid red roses or lilies because of their implications.

## Be Aware of These Gestures

- Personal space among Britons is larger than in the United States. When conversing, don't be surprised if your friend stands farther away than you're accustomed to. Don't step forward to close the gap.
- If your church has folks wearing hats or caps at church services, be prepared to explain why it is allowed. Britons don't wear hats inside churches.
- When visiting the home of a Briton, keep your hands above the table and not on your lap. However, don't put your elbows on the table.
- Don't put your hands in your pockets while talking.
- Pointing with the index finger is considered rude.

## Sensitive Issues

- Avoid discussing the validity of the royal family, and don't make fun of British royalty in any way.
- As with people from most other countries, avoid discussing politics.
- Britons are also reticent to talk about religion. Wait for an appropriate opening or create one.
- Many Britons don't consider themselves Europeans.
- Don't ask personal questions. Britons tend to be very private people.

# 8

# Asia and the Oceanic Region

This chapter provides specific information to help you relate to friends and acquaintances from Asia and countries in the oceanic region. For guidelines on interacting with internationals, please review chapter 5, "General Guidelines for Cross-Cultural Interaction."

## AFGHANISTAN

*Population:* 26.8 million

*Ethnicity:* Pashtun (38 percent), Tajik (25 percent), Hazara (19 percent), Other (12 percent), Uzbek (6 percent)

*Religions/Religious Groups:* Muslim (99 percent), Other (1 percent)

*Languages:* Dari, Pashtu

### How to Greet an Afghan

- Use titles (such as Dr., Professor, Mr., Mrs., and so on) along with the last name of the person. Friends go by first names.
- Handshakes are common. Men should wait for a woman to offer her hand first. However, in traditional Afghan families, it is considered very inappropriate for a woman to shake hands with a man.
- Arabic greetings are common. People usually greet each other by saying *us-sah-lahm ah-lay-kum,* usually responded to by *wah-lay-kum sah-lahm.*

- When leaving, Afghans usually say *khu-dah hah-fizz,* which is equivalent to good-bye.

### Things to Remember When Interacting with an Afghan

- Afghan culture is highly collectivist. This means that most Afghans will consider their acceptance of the gospel in light of how it will impact their family and friends. Chances are you may not get an immediate response. There is also a strong possibility of being disowned by family members if a person changes his or her religion. So be patient and support your Afghan friend if he or she struggles spiritually.
- Most Afghans are Muslims. Read chapter 15 on Islam before trying to witness to an Afghan. Also, Muslims don't eat pork—keep this in mind if you invite an Afghan friend to your house for a meal.
- Afghan culture and heritage, children, and sports are safe topics for conversation. Avoid asking about an Afghan's female relatives.
- Most Afghans in the United States came as refugees. Many of the older generation dream of going back to their homeland someday. However, the younger generation, especially those who were born or raised in the United States, find it difficult to reconcile the two cultures. This has caused much worry and frustration in Afghan families. Consequently, younger Afghans would be more open to the gospel than those from older generations. However, being disowned by the family for forsaking the Islamic faith remains a strong and undesirable possibility for almost all Afghans, young or old. Be sensitive to cross-generational issues.
- A person from Afghanistan is an Afghan, not an "Afghani," which is the unit of money in Afghanistan.

### Be Aware of These Gestures

- Personal space among Afghans is smaller than in the United States. When conversing, don't be surprised if your Afghan friend stands closer than you're accustomed to. Backing away is usually a mistake, as your Afghan friend will simply step forward to close the gap.

- Keep in mind that there is rarely any touching between the sexes (unless they are related).
- If invited to an Afghan home, ask whether you should remove your shoes before entering the house.
- Don't point your feet or shoes at your Afghan friend.
- Don't put your feet on a table or on other furniture.
- The left hand is considered unclean, so avoid using it when eating, shaking hands, or giving and receiving things.

### Sensitive Issues

- Personal honor is of paramount importance to an Afghan. Don't criticize your Afghan friend in front of others.
- Don't initiate conversations about the Taliban, treatment of women in Afghanistan, or poverty and war. If your Afghan friend brings up any of these issues (as is likely), do more listening than talking.
- Avoid discussions about the Israeli-Palestinian conflict.
- Afghans in the United States often feel very vulnerable. Being part of a community, even if it is a church, is a great attraction as long as they are not pressed to make a commitment or decision about Christianity. Concentrate on connecting your Afghan friend with your church, especially outside Sunday services, in settings that are less threatening (i.e., in small groups, at church picnics, at concerts, at plays, at youth activities). Share the gospel, but don't badger for a decision.
- Converting to another religion is almost inconceivable for an Afghan. He or she will most definitely be disowned by his or her family and community.

## AUSTRALIA

*Population:* 19.4 million

*Ethnicity:* Caucasian (92 percent), Asian (7 percent), Aboriginal (1 percent)

*Religions/Religious Groups:* Anglican (26 percent), Roman Catholic (26 percent), Other Christian (24 percent), Other (24 percent)

*Languages:* English and native languages

## *How to Greet an Australian*

- Most Australians are very friendly and outgoing people. A simple "Hello" or "Good Day" (frequently abbreviated to "G'day" and pronounced gid-day) with a handshake is appropriate.
- First names are okay to use unless you are at a formal event.

## *Things to Remember When Interacting with an Australian*

- Australian culture is highly individualistic, which means your Australian friend is free to make his or her own decision about the gospel without a lot of pressure from family members.
- Australians are among the most relaxed and easygoing people in the world.
- A common expression among Australians is "No worries," which means "No problem." Also, men call each other "mate."
- Maintain eye contact, but don't stare.
- Australians tend to be direct in their conversation, so be prepared to talk openly about your beliefs if the opportunity presents itself. But keep in mind that Australians dislike disagreement—be sensitive if your friend appears uncomfortable.
- Australians tend to shorten words (i.e., *uni* for university), so if you don't understand something, ask for an explanation.
- Australians have a great sense of humor and appreciate it in others.
- Australians are very hospitable, and your Australian friend may invite you for "tea." Keep in mind that Australians often refer to dinner as tea.
- If you are invited to an Australian home for a meal, it is customary to bring fruit or homemade goodies. After a meal people stay at the dinner table until everyone has finished.

## *Be Aware of These Gestures*

- The thumbs-up sign is sometimes regarded as an insult.
- Winking at a woman is considered inappropriate.
- Pointing with the index finger is considered rude.
- Yawning in front of others is regarded as impolite.

- Avoid using toothpicks in public.
- The sign for "okay" or "all right" (extending just the thumb and forefinger to make a circle) is viewed as an indignity.
- The *V* for victory sign (the index finger and middle finger with the palm facing in) is considered obscene.

### Sensitive Issues
- Don't compare Australia with the United Kingdom or the United States.
- As in most other countries, politics is a sensitive issue—avoid the topic.
- Avoid initiating or discussing the historical treatment of the Aborigines by the Australian government.

## CHINA
*Population:* 1.273 billion

*Ethnicity:* Han Chinese (92 percent), Other (8 percent)

*Religions/Religious Groups:* Atheist (Atheism is the state "religion"), Taoist, Buddhist, Confucianist, Muslim (No official statistics available. Some estimates say Christians make up about 1 percent of the population.)

*Languages:* Chinese (several forms and dialects)

### How to Greet a Chinese Person
- In China, names are the opposite of the way they are used in Western societies. The family name is used first. For instance, Mr. Chang Ping should be addressed as Mr. Chang. However, this may not be the case with all Chinese in the United States. Some of them take on "English" names such as Stephen or Thomas for everyday use.
- Handshakes are common.
- A common expression is *Chi le ma?* (pronounced chur lur mah), which means "Have you eaten?"—an equivalent to the American greeting "How are you?"

*Speak Mandarin!*

A strong and immediate bridge can be built if you know just a few phrases of your Chinese friend's language. The fact that you took the trouble and made an attempt will mean a lot to your Chinese friend. You will develop rapport almost immediately and, invariably, evoke a smile. The Chinese speak eight major dialects. The most common is Mandarin, which is spoken by about 70 percent of the population in China. Here are some common phrases in Mandarin, which are written as they would be pronounced:*

> Hello: *Knee-how*
> Good-bye: *Zai-jee-an*
> Good morning: *Za-o*
> Good afternoon: *Oo-unn*
> Good evening: *Won-unn*
> How are you? *Knee-how ma?*
> Very well: *Hen how*
> Please: *Ching*
> Thank you: *Shay-shay*

### Things to Remember When Interacting with a Chinese Person

- Chinese culture is highly collectivist. This means that most Chinese will consider their acceptance of the gospel in light of how it will impact their family and friends. Chances are you may not receive an immediate response. There is also a strong possibility of being disowned by family members if a person changes his or her religion. So be patient and support your Chinese friend if he or she struggles spiritually.
- Safe topics for conversation include Chinese culture, hobbies, and family.
- Chinese people tend to be shy and reserved. They are also extremely polite and place great importance on proper etiquette.
- Serving tea to guests is a Chinese custom. (Yes, that's why they offer it in Chinese restaurants!)

---

* Special thanks to Michael and his friend at the Borders bookstore in Germantown, Maryland, for their help with this section.

- If you are invited to a Chinese home, arrive on time or even a little early. Guests usually bring a small gift of fruit or chocolates.
- You will be offered tea. If you have had enough tea, leave your cup about one quarter full. If you eat with chopsticks, make sure you place them on the chopstick rest or on the table after you are done. Placing them *in* your rice bowl is offensive, and placing them parallel *on top of* your bowl is a sign of bad luck.
- After a meal leave a little bit on your plate to signify that you are satisfied. If you don't, your host will think you are still hungry.
- If you hear your Chinese friend making slurping noises, it means he or she is greatly enjoying the meal. Some may even belch loudly to signify satisfaction with the meal. (It is unlikely you will see these signs among Chinese who have been in America for a while.)
- Keep in mind that some Chinese practice multiple religions.
- Be prepared for personal questions.

### Be Aware of These Gestures
- If you are invited to a Chinese home, ask whether you should remove your shoes before entering the house.
- Use both hands when receiving or giving things.
- Avoid physical contact of any kind (other than handshakes). Chinese people don't like physical contact with strangers.
- Don't use your index finger to point at things. The Chinese use their hands to point at things.

### Sensitive Issues
- As is the case with people from most other countries, avoid discussions about politics.
- Don't get into conversations about communism unless your Chinese friend initiates the discussion. Even then, do more listening than talking.
- Don't ever give a gift of a clock, straws, or handkerchiefs—they are associated with funerals.

- Don't criticize your Chinese friend in front of others; this will cause him or her to lose face (become humiliated).
- Don't make fun of Chinese dragons or customs.
- Don't get into discussions about Hong Kong and Taiwan.
- Avoid the topic of Tibet.

## INDIA

*Population:* 1.03 billion

*Ethnicity:* Indo-Aryan (72 percent), Dravidian (25 percent), Other (3 percent)

*Religions/Religious Groups:* Hindu (80 percent), Muslim (14 percent), Other— including Buddhist, Jain, Parsi, Sikh, and Christian (6 percent)

*Languages:* English, Hindi, Bengali, Telegu, Marathi, Tamil, Urdu, Gujarati, Malayalam, Kannada, Oriya, Punjabi, Assamese, Kashmiri, Sindhi, Sanskrit, and hundreds of other languages and dialects

### How to Greet an Indian

- Use titles (such as Dr., Professor, Mr., Mrs., and so on) along with the last name of the person. Friends use first names.
- Handshakes are common, although men should wait for a woman to offer her hand first.
- A common form of greeting in India is to put the palms together, place them at chest level, bow slightly, and say *"Namaste"* (pronounced nah-mus-tay).

### Speak Hindi!

A strong and immediate bridge can be built with your Indian friend if you know just a few phrases in his or her language. The fact that you took the trouble and made an attempt will mean a lot. You will develop rapport almost immediately and, invariably, evoke a smile. Although hundreds of languages and dialects are used in India, most Indians can speak English and/or Hindi. Here are some common phrases in Hindi:

Hello/Good-bye: *Namaste* (nah-mus-tay)

Good morning/afternoon/evening/night: *Namaste* (nah-mus-tay)

How are you? *Aap kaise ho?* (ahp kai-say ho?)

I am fine: *Mein thik hoon* (may theek hoo)

Please: *Kripya* (krip-yah)

Thank you: *Dhanyabad* (dhan-yah-bahd) or *Shukriya* (shook-ree-yah)

Yes: *Haa* (hah)

No: *Naa* (nah) or *Nuh-hee*

### Things to Remember When Interacting with an Indian

- Indian culture is highly collectivist. This means that most Indians will consider their acceptance of the gospel in light of how it will impact their family and friends. Chances are you may not receive an immediate response. There is also a strong possibility of being disowned by family members if a person changes his or her religion. So be prepared to support your Indian friend if he or she struggles spiritually.

- Safe topics of conversation include Indian culture and heritage. Cricket and football (soccer) are among the most popular sports.

- Most Indians are either Hindus or Muslims. Keep in mind that Hindus don't eat beef and Muslims don't eat pork. Most Hindus are vegetarians. Also, since the cow is sacred in India and most leather products are made from cowhide, any such gifts are out of the question for devout Hindus.

- You might see a child bowing and touching his or her parents' feet. This is an age-old practice of showing respect to one's elders.

- Indian food tends to be spicy and hot. If invited to an Indian home, you may want to find out if a particular dish is hot by trying a small amount before taking more. Also, you will find your Indian host or hostess will ask you several times to have more food even after you say you are full. Don't take offense, as this is a common Indian custom to make sure a guest is truly satisfied.

- Most Indians eat with their hands, although this is not as common among Indians in the United States.

- Hospitality is highly prized in Indian culture. Hindus consider it a spiritually rewarding experience to entertain guests.

- Because Indians come from a collectivist society and yearn for community, many will be open to coming with you to church if it means being part of a community where people are genuinely concerned about one another.

## *Be Aware of These Gestures*

- If invited to an Indian home, ask whether you should remove your shoes before entering the house. It is okay to bring chocolates or flowers, but avoid red roses because of their implications. Also, it is customary to wash your hands before and after a meal.
- Sometimes an Indian may shake his or her head side to side to indicate understanding or affirmation—or up and down to indicate a negative response (exactly the opposite of how these gestures are viewed here in America).
- The left hand is considered unclean, so avoid using it when eating, shaking hands, or giving and receiving things.
- Don't point your feet at someone.
- Touching one's ears is a sign of embarrassment or remorse.

## *Sensitive Issues*

- As is the case with people from most other countries, avoid discussions about politics.
- Don't touch or lean on any idols of gods and goddesses that you might see at an Indian friend's house.
- Don't put your feet on top of books or magazines. Indians (especially Hindus) revere printed literature as a source of wisdom. To deliberately mishandle them is to dishonor wisdom. Letting your feet touch the Bible or flinging it around is a sure way to turn off an Indian. He or she will think that if Christians don't respect their own Scriptures, they probably don't mean much to them.
- Avoid questions that may have a negative answer. Indians generally dislike saying no. If you invite an Indian friend to a church event, and he or she replies, "Good," you may think that your friend will be there.

But if your friend does not really want to go, he or she will simply not show up and then will avoid you completely in the future. Instead, try asking, "What are you doing on Sunday morning?" If your friend doesn't have any plans, then say, "I would love to have you come and join us for our church service this Sunday or any Sunday you are free. Just let me know." This gives your friend the option of deciding whether he or she wants to go and allows him or her an "out" without actually having to say no.

- Don't criticize your Indian friend in front of others; this will cause him or her to lose face (become humiliated).
- Don't get into conversations about personal issues.
- Don't make fun of Indian customs or Hindu gods and goddesses. Don't make fun of the fact that Hindus consider the cow a sacred animal.
- Avoid discussions about the India-Pakistan conflict.
- Don't talk about poverty in India.

## INDONESIA

*Population:* 228.4 million

*Ethnicity:* Javanese (45 percent), Other (25 percent), Sundanese (14 percent), Madurese (8 percent), Coastal Malays (8 percent)

*Religions/Religious Groups:* Muslim (87 percent), Protestant (6 percent), Other—including Roman Catholic, Hindu, and Buddhist (7 percent)

*Languages:* Bahasa Indonesia, English, Dutch, and local dialects

### How to Greet an Indonesian

- Use titles (such as Dr., Professor, Mr., Mrs., and so on) along with the last name of the person. Friends use first names.
- Handshakes are common, although men should wait for a woman to offer her hand first.

### Speak Bahasa Indonesia!

A strong and immediate bridge can be built if you know just a few phrases of your Indonesian friend's language. The fact that you took the trouble and made an attempt will mean a lot to your Indonesian friend. You will develop rapport almost immediately and, invariably, evoke a smile. Here are some common phrases in Bahasa Indonesia, which are written as they would be pronounced:

Hello: *Hah-lo*

Good-bye: *Sir-lah-mat ting-gahl*

Good morning: *Sir-lah-mat puh-gee*

Good afternoon: *Sir-lah-mat see-ang*

Good evening: *Sir-lah-mat sore*

Good night: *Sir-lah-mat muh-lam*

Please: *Toh-long*

Thank you: *Ter-ri-mah kah-see*

Yes: *Yah*

No: *Tee-dahk*

### *Things to Remember When Interacting with an Indonesian*

- Indonesian culture is highly collectivist. This means that most Indonesians will consider their acceptance of the gospel in light of how it will impact their family and friends. Chances are you may not receive an immediate response. There is also a strong possibility of being disowned by family members if a person changes his or her religion. Be patient and support your Indonesian friend if he or she struggles spiritually.
- Learn your Indonesian friend's name and how to pronounce it correctly. Names are considered sacred in Indonesia, so pronouncing them correctly is important.
- Most Indonesians are Muslims. Read chapter 15 on Islam before trying to witness to an Indonesian. Also, Muslims don't eat pork—keep this in mind if you invite an Indonesian friend to your house for a meal.
- Indonesians are friendly and hospitable.
- Safe topics of conversation include Indonesian culture and sports (soccer and tennis are popular sports).
- Indonesians shy away from conflict and will avoid topics of conversation they feel will result in disagreements. Pray for guidance in creatively witnessing to your Indonesian friend.

- If invited to an Indonesian home for a meal, leave a little bit of food on your plate to indicate you have enjoyed the meal. You may experience considerable periods of silence while eating. This is normal; Indonesians usually don't talk during meals.
- Rice, vegetables, and fish are popular food items.

## Be Aware of These Gestures

- If invited to an Indonesian home, ask whether you should remove your shoes before entering the house.
- Pointing with the index finger is considered rude.
- Chewing gum while talking is regarded as rude.
- Don't touch the head of an Indonesian (not even a child's head); it is considered to be the place where the spirit lives.
- The left hand is considered unclean, so avoid using it when eating, shaking hands, or giving and receiving things.
- Don't touch anything with your feet.
- Try not to yawn in front of your Indonesian friend. If you have to yawn, cover your mouth.
- When visiting an Indonesian home, keep your hands above the table and not on your lap. However, don't put your elbows on the table.

## Sensitive Issues

- Never criticize your Indonesian friend or his or her beliefs in front of others. This causes him or her to feel *malu* (pronounced mah-loo), which means to lose face or become humiliated.
- Never embarrass your Indonesian friend—being embarrassed is considered a great insult.
- Showing anger is considered offensive.
- As with people from most other countries, avoid discussions about politics.
- Avoid asking personal questions or criticizing Indonesian culture.

- Don't point the bottom of your feet or shoes toward your Indonesian friend.
- Avoid questions that may have a negative answer. Indonesians dislike saying no. If you invite an Indonesian friend to a church event, and he or she replies, "Good," you may think that your friend will be there. But if your friend does not really want to go, he or she will simply not show up and then will avoid you completely in the future. Instead, try asking, "What are you doing Sunday morning?" If your friend doesn't have any plans, then say, "I would love to have you come and join us for our church service this Sunday or any Sunday you are free. Just let me know." This gives your friend the option of deciding whether he or she wants to go and allows him or her an "out" without actually having to say no.

## JAPAN
*Population:* 126.8 million
*Ethnicity:* Japanese (99.4 percent), Other (0.6 percent)
*Religions/Religious Groups:* Shintoist and Buddhist (84 percent), Other (16 percent)
*Language:* Japanese

### How to Greet a Japanese Person
- Use titles (such as Dr., Professor, Mr., Mrs., and so on) along with the last name of the person. Friends use first names.
- The traditional form of greeting is the bow. However, it is rarely used by the Japanese when greeting an American here in the United States (unless they are tourists or have been here for a very short time). Handshakes are common.

### Speak Japanese!
A strong and immediate bridge can be built with your Japanese friend if you know just a few phrases of the Japanese language. The fact that you took the

trouble and made an attempt will mean a lot. You will develop rapport almost immediately and, invariably, evoke a smile. Here are some common phrases in Japanese, which are written as they would be pronounced:

Hello: *Koh-nee-chee wah*

Good-bye: *Sah-yo-nah-rah*

Good morning: *Oh-hi-yo go-zee-mass*

Good afternoon: *Koh-nee-chee wah*

Good evening: *Comb-bahn wah*

How are you? *Oh-gen-kee dess kah?*

I am fine: *Gen-kee dess*

Please: *Doh-zoh*

Thank you: *Doh-moh ah-ree-gah-toh*

Yes: *Hai*

No: *Iee*

### *Things to Remember When Interacting with a Japanese Person*

- Japanese culture is highly collectivist. This means that most Japanese people will consider their acceptance of the gospel in light of how it will impact their family and friends. Chances are you may not get an immediate response. There is also a strong possibility of being disowned by family members if a person changes his or her religion. For most Japanese, family is more important than religion. Be patient and support your Japanese friend if he or she struggles spiritually.
- Safe topics of conversation include Japanese culture and food. Sports (including baseball and golf) is also a popular subject.
- The Japanese place a lot of importance on relationships. If the Lord leads you to witness to a Japanese person, don't expect it to be a one-time encounter. In order to be effective, you will need to build a relationship over a period of time. Only then will your words have credibility.
- The Japanese way of conversing is often vague rather than direct. You may have an opportunity to witness extensively, but you may find it

hard to figure out exactly how your Japanese friend views the gospel. This is why building a relationship is so important.

- If you are invited to a Japanese home, it is customary to bring cake, fruits, or flowers—although you should bring only odd numbers of flowers (except one or thirteen). Avoid red roses because of romantic implications or white flowers, which are associated with death.
- If invited to a Japanese friend's home, remember that eating is seen as a ritual and a time for interaction. Allow plenty of time. If soup is served, don't finish it right away; it is an accompaniment to the entire meal. If you eat with chopsticks, make sure you place them on the chopstick rest or on the table after you are done. Leave some food on your plate or in your bowl to signify that you are full or satisfied.
- If you hear your Japanese friend making slurping noises, it means he or she is greatly enjoying the meal. Some Japanese may even belch loudly to signify satisfaction with the meal. (It is unlikely you will see these signs among Japanese people who have been in the United States for a while.)
- The Japanese culture values education, so if your church or a local Christian organization offers a course in English (or other courses), it would probably be a good place to invite your Japanese friend.
- The Japanese are often silent between conversations. Don't rush to fill the silence. Wait for a few moments to make sure your Japanese friend has finished talking before you reply.
- The Japanese have deep respect for elderly people. Age is revered.

### Be Aware of These Gestures
- If invited to a Japanese home, ask whether you should remove your shoes before entering the house.
- The sign for "okay" or "all right" (extending just the thumb and forefinger to make a circle) means "money" to Japanese people.
- Try not to yawn in front of your Japanese friend. If you have to yawn, cover your mouth.

- Chewing gum while talking is regarded as rude.
- Pointing with the index finger is considered rude. Use your entire hand to point.
- Don't put your feet on a table or on other furniture.
- Use both hands when receiving and giving things.
- Don't put your hands in your pockets while talking.

### Sensitive Issues

- Most Japanese people are extremely polite and value politeness.
- To the Japanese, patience is a great virtue, so expect your dialogue about the gospel to cover a period of time. Concentrate on building a relationship with your Japanese friend.
- Saving face is of utmost importance, so don't criticize a Japanese person or his or her beliefs in public.
- Avoid questions that may have a negative answer. The Japanese dislike saying no. If you invite a Japanese friend to a church event, and he or she replies, "Good," you may think your friend will be there. But if your friend does not really want to go, he or she will simply not show up and then will avoid you completely in the future. Instead, try asking, "What are you doing Sunday morning?" If your friend doesn't have any plans, then say, "I would love to have you join us for our church service this Sunday or any Sunday you are free. Just let me know." This gives your friend the option of deciding whether he or she wants to go and allows him or her an "out" without actually having to say no.
- Avoid talking about World War II.
- Don't be surprised if your Japanese friend asks you a lot of personal questions. This is considered acceptable in Japan. Be prepared for them.

## MALAYSIA

*Population:* 22.2 million

*Ethnicity:* Malay and Other Indigenous Groups (58 percent), Chinese (26 percent), Indian (7 percent), Other (9 percent)

*Religions/Religious Groups:* Muslim, Buddhist, Hindu, Christian, Sikh
   (no official statistics available)
*Languages:* Bahasa Melayu, English, Chinese dialects, Tamil, Telegu,
   Malayalam, Punjabi, Thai, and several indigenous languages

### How to Greet a Malaysian

- A common form of greeting is to touch the other person's outstretched
  hands with both your hands lightly and quickly and then to touch your
  chest. This means you are greeting the person from your heart. Another
  common form of greeting is *"Halo"* (pronounced hah-loh), which
  means "Hello."
- Handshakes are common, although men should wait for a woman to
  offer her hand first.

### Speak Malay!

A strong and immediate bridge can be built with your Malaysian friend if you
know just a few phrases of his or her language. The fact that you took the trouble
and made an attempt will mean a lot. You will develop rapport almost immediately and, invariably, evoke a smile. Here are some common phrases in Malay (officially known as Bahasa Melayu), which are written as they would be pronounced:

   Hello: *Seh-lah-maht tehn-gah-ha-ree*
   Good-bye: *Seh-lah-maht ting-gahl* (if you are leaving); *Seh-lah-maht
      jah-lahn* (if someone else is leaving)
   Good morning: *Seh-lah-maht pah-gee*
   Good afternoon: *Seh-lah-maht peh-tahng*
   Good evening/night: *Seh-lah-maht mah-lahm*
   How are you? *Ah-peh kah-bahr?*
   I am fine, thanks: *Kah-bahr bah-eek*
   Please: *To-lohng*
   Thank you: *Teh-ree-mah kah-say*
   Yes: *Yah*
   No: *Tee-dahk*

## *Things to Remember When Interacting with a Malaysian*

- Malaysian culture is collectivist. This means that most Malaysians will consider their acceptance of the gospel in light of how it will impact their family and friends. Chances are you may not get an immediate response, so be patient and support your Malaysian friend if he or she struggles spiritually.

- Safe topics of conversation include Malaysian culture, food, and sports (soccer is the most popular sport).

- Relationships are important. You may have to build a relationship with your Malaysian friend and share the gospel over a period of time.

- The Malaysian people place a lot of importance on maintaining harmony among family, friends, and others. For this reason they avoid conflicts or topics of conversation that may result in disagreements.

- Malaysians love children, so one good way to bring the gospel into your conversation is to mention what the Bible says about children.

- Malaysians view Americans as materialistic. To them, family, friends, and relatives are more important than material success. A Malaysian may ask, "If things are *not* more important than people, then why do most Americans have *more* things than people in their lives?" or "Why is there a lack of real community?" Be prepared to answer these questions from your own perspective.

- Since Muslims don't eat pork and Hindus and Buddhists don't eat beef (most Malaysians follow one of these religions), be careful not to serve beef or pork when inviting a Malaysian friend for a meal. Rice and fish are popular in the Malaysian diet.

- Malaysians traditionally refuse an offer when it is first made. If you are offering your Malaysian friend something, repeat the offer to make sure he or she has a chance to say yes.

- Malaysians are often silent during their conversations. Don't rush to fill any silences. Wait for a few moments to make sure your Malaysian friend has finished talking before replying.

- After a meal don't leave any food on your plate. It is considered rude.

*Be Aware of These Gestures*

- If invited to a Malaysian home, ask whether you should remove your shoes before entering the house.
- Don't touch a Malaysian's head (not even a child's)—the head is considered holy and sacred.
- Pointing with the index finger is considered rude. Malaysians often use the thumb (with fingers folded) to point at things.
- Don't put your hands in your pockets while talking.
- The left hand is considered unclean, so avoid using it when eating, shaking hands, or giving and receiving things.
- Don't point your feet or shoes at your Malaysian friend. Don't put your feet on furniture.

*Sensitive Issues*

- Don't talk about the intermittent conflict between Malaysia and China.
- As is the case with people from most other countries, avoid discussions about politics.
- Avoid questions that may have a negative answer. Malaysians dislike saying no. If you invite a Malaysian friend to a church event, and he or she replies, "Good," you may think that your friend will be there. But if your friend does not really want to go, he or she will simply not show up and then will avoid you completely in the future. Instead, try asking, "What are you doing Sunday morning?" If your friend doesn't have any plans, then say, "I would love to have you come and join us for our church service this Sunday or any Sunday you are free. Just let me know." This gives your friend the option of deciding whether he or she wants to go and allows him or her an "out" without actually having to say no.
- Don't compare Malaysia with the United States.
- Don't criticize your Malaysian friend in front of others, as this will cause him or her to lose face (become humiliated).
- The role of the sexes in Malaysian culture is another taboo topic.
- Be prepared to be asked personal questions.

## NEW ZEALAND

*Population:* 3.9 million

*Ethnicity:* New Zealand European (75 percent), Other (15 percent), Maori (10 percent)

*Religions/Religious Groups:* Other (43 percent), Protestant—Presbyterian (18 percent), Anglican (24 percent), Roman Catholic (15 percent)

*Languages:* English and Maori

### How to Greet a New Zealander

- A common form of greeting is "Good day" (pronounced gid-day).
- Handshakes are common, although men should wait for a woman to offer her hand first. A bit of interesting trivia is that the traditional greeting among the Maori people (12 percent of the New Zealand population) is to rub noses. Avoid using this particular greeting!

### Things to Remember When Interacting with a New Zealander

- New Zealand culture is highly individualistic, which means your New Zealander friend is free to make his or her own decision about the gospel without a lot of pressure from family members.
- If you are invited to the home of a New Zealander, it is okay to bring chocolates or flowers, but don't give red roses because of the romantic implications.
- Safe topics of conversation include hobbies and sports (soccer and rugby are among the most popular sports).
- Your New Zealander friend may refer to his or her countrymen as Kiwis.
- Unlike people from most other countries, New Zealanders tend to be *early* for appointments.
- New Zealanders tend to be easygoing and relaxed.
- New Zealanders are hospitable, and your friend may invite you for "tea." Keep in mind that New Zealanders often use the word *tea* to mean dinner.

## Be Aware of These Gestures

- If invited to the home of a New Zealander, keep your hands above the table and not on your lap. However, don't put your elbows on the table.
- Chewing gum while talking is regarded as rude behavior.
- Avoid using toothpicks in public.
- The *V* for victory sign (with the index finger and the middle finger with the palm facing inward) is considered obscene.

## Sensitive Issues

- Avoid talking about racial issues between the Maori and European New Zealanders.
- As with people from most other countries, avoid discussing politics. If your New Zealander friend broaches the topic, do more listening than talking.
- Don't confuse or compare New Zealand with Australia. Many New Zealanders resent being lumped together with Australians.

## PAKISTAN

*Population:* 144.6 million

*Ethnicity:* Punjabi, Sindhi, Pashtun, Mujahir, Baloch (no official statistics available)

*Religions/Religious Groups:* Muslim (97 percent), Other—including Christian and Hindu (3 percent)

*Languages:* Punjabi, Sindhi, Siraika, Pashtu, Urdu, and several other languages and dialects.

## How to Greet a Pakistani

- Use titles (such as Dr., Professor, Mr., Mrs., and so on) along with the last name of the person. Friends use first names.
- Handshakes are common among men. Men should wait for a woman to offer her hand first. However, in traditional Pakistani families, it is considered very inappropriate for a woman to shake hands with a man.

*Things to Remember When Interacting with a Pakistani*

- Pakistani culture is highly collectivist. This means that most Pakistanis will consider their acceptance of the gospel in light of how it will impact their family and friends. Chances are you may not get an immediate response. There is also a strong possibility of being disowned by family members if a Pakistani changes his or her religion. So be patient and support your Pakistani friend if he or she struggles spiritually.
- Safe topics of conversation include Pakistani culture, music, and sports. (Soccer, cricket, and hockey are among the most popular sports.)
- Most Pakistanis are Muslims. Read chapter 15 on Islam before trying to witness to a Pakistani. Also, Muslims don't eat pork—keep this in mind if you invite a Pakistani friend to your house for a meal.
- Pakistani food tends to be hot and spicy. If invited to a Pakistani home, find out if a particular dish is hot, then take a little and taste it before taking more. Also, your Pakistani host or hostess is likely to ask you several times if you would like more food, even after you say you are full. Don't take offense, as this is a common Pakistani custom to make sure a guest is truly satisfied.
- Most Pakistanis eat with their hands, although this is not as common among Pakistanis in the United States.
- Pakistanis yearn for community; thus, many will be open to coming to church if it means being part of a community where people are genuinely concerned about one another.

*Be Aware of These Gestures*

- If invited to a Pakistani home, ask whether you should remove your shoes before entering the house.
- The left hand is considered unclean, so avoid using it when eating, shaking hands, or giving and receiving things.
- Don't point the bottom of your feet or the soles of your shoes toward a Pakistani.

- Winking, especially at someone of the opposite sex, is considered highly inappropriate.

### Sensitive Issues

- As is the case with people from most other countries, avoid discussions about politics.
- Some Pakistanis consider dogs to be unclean animals.
- Don't initiate conversations about personal issues.
- Avoid discussions regarding the India-Pakistan or the Israeli-Palestinian conflicts.
- Don't talk about poverty or the standard of living in Pakistan.
- Avoid comparing Pakistan with the United States or India.

## PHILIPPINES

*Population:* 82.8 million

*Ethnicity:* Christian Malay (92 percent), Muslim Malay (4 percent), Other (4 percent)

*Religions/Religious Groups:* Roman Catholic (83 percent), Protestant (9 percent), Muslim (5 percent), Other (3 percent)

*Languages:* Tagalog, English, and eight other major dialects

### How to Greet a Filipino

- Use titles (such as Dr., Professor, Mr., Mrs., and so on) along with the last name of the person. Friends use first names.
- Handshakes are common, although men should wait for a woman to offer her hand first.

### Speak Tagalog!

A strong and immediate bridge can be built with your Filipino friend if you know just a few phrases in his or her language. The fact that you took the trouble and made an attempt will mean a lot. You will develop rapport almost immediately and, invariably, evoke a smile. Here are some common phrases in Tagalog:

Hello: *Kamusta* (kah-moos-tah)

Good-bye: *Paalam* (pah-lahm)

Good morning: *Magandang umaga* (mah-gahn-dang oo-mah-gah)

Good afternoon: *Magandang hapon* (mah-gahn-dang hah-pawn)

Good evening: *Magandang gabi* (mah-gahn-dang gah-bee)

How are you? *Kumusta ho kayo?* (koo-moos-tah ho kah-yoh?)

Fine: *Mabuti naman* (mah-boo-tee nah-mahn)

Thank you: *Salamat* (sah-lah-maht)

Yes: *Oo* (ooh)

No: *Hindi* (heen-dee)

### *Things to Remember When Interacting with a Filipino*

- Filipino culture is highly collectivist. This means that most Filipinos will consider their acceptance of the gospel in light of how it will impact their family and friends. Chances are you may not get an immediate response, so be patient and support your Filipino friend if he or she struggles spiritually.
- Safe topics of conversation include families, Filipino culture, movies, and sports (basketball is a very popular sport in the Philippines).
- Hospitality and friendliness characterize the Filipino culture. In fact, Filipinos create an atmosphere of friendliness wherever they go.
- Filipinos tend to agree in order to avoid confrontations. Although this makes it easier to invite Filipinos to church, actual decisions about Christ may not come quickly and could require several discussions over a period of time.
- Family is more important than the individual. Hence, when you witness to a Filipino, he or she may seem convinced but may not make a decision for fear of being alienated from his or her family.
- Relationships are important. You may have to build a relationship with your Filipino friend and talk about your faith in Christ over a period of time.
- Filipinos tend to be sensitive, and most Filipinos believe in fate.

- If you are invited to a Filipino home, it is okay to bring chocolates or flowers, but avoid red roses because of romantic implications.
- After a meal leave a little bit of food on your plate to signify that you are satisfied. If you don't, your host will think you are still hungry.

## Be Aware of These Gestures

- Raising eyebrows is considered a yes.
- Most Filipinos use their eyes rather than their hands or fingers to point at things.

## Sensitive Issues

- As with people from most other countries, avoid discussing politics.
- Saving face is of utmost importance, so don't criticize a Filipino or his or her beliefs in front of others.
- Like the Japanese, Filipinos dislike saying no, so avoid questions that may have a negative answer. If you invite a Filipino friend to a church event, and he or she replies, "Good," you may think that your friend will be there. But if your friend does not really want to go, he or she will simply not show up and then will avoid you completely in the future. Instead, try asking, "What are you doing on Sunday morning?" If your friend doesn't have any plans, then say, "I would love to have you come and join us for our church service this Sunday or any Sunday you are free. Just let me know." This gives your friend the option of deciding whether he or she wants to go and allows him or her an "out" without actually having to say no.

## SOUTH KOREA

*Population:* 47.9 million

*Ethnicity:* Largely homogeneous

*Religions/Religious Groups:* Christian (49 percent), Buddhist (47 percent), Confucianist (3 percent), Other (1 percent)

*Languages:* Korean and English

## How to Greet a Korean

- Use titles (such as Dr., Professor, Mr., Mrs., and so on) along with the family name of the person. Friends go by their last name. Keep in mind that the family name or the last name always comes first. For example, Mr. Kim Sam should be addressed as Mr. Kim.
- Handshakes are common, although men should wait for a woman to offer her hand first. A slight bow is appropriate.
- A common form of greeting is *"Annyong haseyo?"* (pronounced ahn-yong hah-say-o), which means "Are you at peace?"

## Speak Korean!

A strong and immediate bridge can be built with your Korean friend if you know just a few phrases in his or her language. The fact that you took the trouble and made an attempt will mean a lot. You will develop rapport almost immediately and, invariably, evoke a smile. Here are some common phrases in Korean, which are written as they would be pronounced:

Hello: *Yo-bo-say-yo*

Good-bye: *An-yong-hi kah-ship-shi-yo*

Good morning/afternoon/night: *An-yong-hah-shim-nee-kah*

Thank you: *Kam-sah-ham-ni-dah*

Please: *Jay-bahl*

## Things to Remember When Interacting with a Korean

- Korean culture is highly collectivist. This means most Koreans will consider their acceptance of the gospel in light of how it will impact their family and friends. You may not get an immediate response, so be patient and support your Korean friend if he or she struggles spiritually.
- Safe topics of conversation include Korean culture, hobbies, kite flying, and sports. Soccer and basketball are popular sports. The martial art *tae kwon do* comes from Korea and is also quite popular.
- In Korea there is great respect for the elderly. One's parents and grandparents are shown the utmost respect and honor, and Koreans are often

shocked at the way older people are treated in America. Showing disrespect to the elderly, sending older members of the family to nursing homes, and openly disagreeing with them are often seen as brutal and cruel acts. Be prepared to discuss this topic if it ever comes up and explain why it is this way in America.

- Koreans are considered to be among the most polite people on earth.
- It is okay to praise your Korean friend. Unlike many other Asian cultures, giving and receiving praise is a way of life among Koreans. However, expect your Korean friend to deny any compliments you do give.
- Be careful not to praise an object too much, or your friend may end up giving it to you!
- If you are invited to a Korean home, it is okay to bring fruit or chocolates.
- If you eat with chopsticks, make sure you place them on the chopstick rest or on the table after you are done. If you are served rice, it is okay to use a spoon. Leave a little bit of food on your plate to signify that you are satisfied. If you don't, your host will think you are still hungry.
- If invited to a Korean social gathering, be prepared to sing! Everyone is expected to sing, and if you are asked, do so. This will create a strong rapport with your Korean friends.

### Be Aware of These Gestures
- If invited to a Korean home, ask whether you should remove your shoes before entering the house.
- Unlike many countries in the world, in Korea men often have the privilege of being first. Men enter through doors first, sit first, walk in front of women, and so on. It is not unusual to see a Korean woman helping her husband with his coat.
- Touching another person—if you don't know him or her very well—can be seen as an insult.

- Avoid putting a hand on your Korean friend's back or shoulder unless you know him or her very well.
- If your Korean friend smacks his or her lips after a meal, it means he or she greatly enjoyed the meal. Some Koreans may even belch loudly to signify satisfaction with the meal. (It is unlikely you will see these signs among Koreans who have been in the United States for a while.)
- Use both hands when receiving or giving things.
- Don't place your feet on furniture.
- If your Korean friend laughs a lot, it may be a sign that he or she is embarrassed.

### Sensitive Issues

- As with people from most other countries, avoid discussing politics.
- Some Koreans may ask you personal questions. Be cautious in how you respond to them.
- Avoid any kind of physical contact.
- Keep in mind that a yes may not always mean agreement.
- Showing anger is considered impolite.
- Don't ever confuse Koreans with Japanese.
- Don't criticize anything Korean.
- Don't criticize your Korean friend in front of others; this will cause him or her to lose face (become humiliated).
- Never make your Korean friend the receiving end of jokes. It will be remembered and highly resented.
- Avoid initiating discussions about communism or Japan. Other taboo topics include the Korean War.
- Also, if you are a male interacting with a Korean male, don't inquire about your Korean friend's female relatives.

## SRI LANKA

*Population:* 19.4 million

*Ethnicity:* Sinhalese (74 percent), Tamil (18 percent), Moor (7 percent), Other (1 percent)

*Religions/Religious Groups:* Buddhist (69 percent), Hindu (15 percent),
   Christian (8 percent), Muslim (8 percent)
*Languages:* Sinhala and Tamil

## How to Greet a Sri Lankan
- Use titles (such as Dr., Professor, Mr., Mrs., and so on) along with the last name of the person. Friends use first names.
- As in India, a common form of greeting in Sri Lanka is to put the palms together, place them at chest level, bow slightly, and say, *"Namaste"* (pronounced nah-mus-tay).
- Handshakes are common, although men should wait for a woman to offer her hand first.

## Things to Remember When Interacting with a Sri Lankan
- Sri Lankan culture is collectivist. This means that most Sri Lankans will consider their acceptance of the gospel in light of how it will impact their family and friends. Chances are you may not get an immediate response, so be patient and support your Sri Lankan friend if he or she struggles spiritually.
- Good topics for conversation include hobbies, families, and sports.
- Sri Lankans are friendly and hard-working people.
- Most Sri Lankans are Buddhists or Hindus. Read chapter 14 on Hinduism and chapter 17 on Buddhism before sharing the gospel with a Sri Lankan. Also, Muslims don't eat pork, and Hindus and Buddhists don't eat beef. Keep this in mind if you invite a Sri Lankan friend to your house for a meal.

## Be Aware of These Gestures
- If invited to a Sri Lankan home, ask whether you should remove your shoes before entering the house. If invited for a meal, take a small helping the first time and then take a second helping—this would be a great compliment to your hosts.

- Sometimes a Sri Lankan may shake his or her head side to side to indicate understanding or affirmation—or up and down to indicate a negative response (exactly the opposite of how these gestures are viewed in America).
- Don't touch or lean on any idols of Buddha you might see at a Sri Lankan friend's house.
- The left hand is considered unclean, so avoid using it when eating, shaking hands, or giving and receiving things.
- Pointing with the index finger is considered rude.
- Don't touch anyone's head (not even a child's). It is considered sacred.
- Don't point your feet or shoes at your Sri Lankan friend.
- Don't put your feet on a table or on other furniture.

### Sensitive Issues
- As in most other countries, politics is a sensitive issue. Avoid political discussions—especially relations with India and the conflict with the Tamils.
- Don't criticize your Sri Lankan friend in front of others; this would cause him or her to lose face (become humiliated).
- Sri Lankans tend to be indirect in their communication. Ask open-ended questions. Just because a person smiles or verbally agrees with you doesn't mean he or she actually agrees!

### THAILAND
*Population:* 61.8 million
*Ethnicity:* Thai (75 percent), Chinese (14 percent), Other (11 percent)
*Religions/Religious Groups:* Buddhist (95 percent), Muslim (4 percent), Other (1 percent)
*Languages:* Thai, English, and several ethnic and regional dialects

### How to Greet a Thai
- Use titles (such as Dr., Professor, Mr., Mrs., and so on) along with the

first name of the person. Friends use first names. Your Thai friend will probably prefer a first-name basis quite soon.

- Handshakes are common, although men should wait for a woman to offer her hand first. However, the traditional Thai greeting is the *wai*—the hands are clasped together (palms facing each other) and held in front of the chest. This is accompanied with a slight bow. It is similar to the Indian *namaste*.

### Speak Thai!

A strong and immediate bridge can be built with your Thai friend if you know just a few phrases in his or her language. The fact that you took the trouble and made an attempt will mean a lot. You will develop rapport almost immediately and, invariably, evoke a smile. Here are some common phrases in Thai, which are written as they would be pronounced:

Hello: *Sah-wat-dee*

Good-bye: *Sah-waht-dee*

Good morning/afternoon/evening: *Sah-wat-dee*

How are you? *Pen yang gai?*

Fine: *Sah-bahy-deh*

Please: *Gah-roo-nah*

Thank you: *Khaup-koon*

Yes: *Crape* (men); *Kah* (women)

No: *Mai*

### Things to Remember When Interacting with a Thai

- Thai culture is collectivist. This means that most Thais will consider their acceptance of the gospel in light of how it will impact their family and friends. Chances are you may not get an immediate response, so be patient and supportive of your Thai friend if he or she struggles spiritually.
- Most Thais are Buddhists. Read chapter 17 on Buddhism before trying to witness to a Thai. Also, Buddhists don't eat beef, so

keep this in mind if you invite a Thai friend to your house for a meal.

- Safe topics of conversation include Thai culture and sports (soccer and table tennis are among the most popular sports). Thai royalty is another great topic for conversation as long as you don't ridicule it.
- Thais tend to talk in a low voice and dislike loud behavior.
- Your Thai friend may ask you personal questions, so be prepared for them.
- If you are invited to a Thai home, it is customary to bring cake or flowers—although you should bring only odd numbers of flowers (except one or thirteen). Avoid red roses (because of their romantic implications), marigolds, and carnations (they are used in funerals).
- Most Thais use chopsticks only for noodles. Rice and other entrées are often eaten with a fork or a spoon.

### Be Aware of These Gestures
- If invited to a Thai home, ask whether you should remove your shoes before entering the house. Also, be sure to walk *over* the threshold rather than *on* it. Most Thais believe souls live in the thresholds of homes.
- Don't touch or lean on any idols of Buddha you might see at a Thai friend's house. Also, don't say anything that could be interpreted as making fun of the picture of Thai royalty.
- Don't touch a Thai's head (not even a child's); it is considered sacred.
- Don't cross your legs while sitting down.
- Pointing with the index finger can be seen as rude. Use your hand instead.
- Don't point the bottom of your feet or your shoes at a Thai.

- Keeping your hands in your pockets while talking is considered rude.
- The left hand is considered unclean, so avoid using it when eating, shaking hands, or giving and receiving things.

### Sensitive Issues

- Avoid questions that may have a negative answer. Thais dislike saying no. If you invite a Thai friend to a church event, and he or she replies, "Good," you may think that your friend will be there. But if your friend does not really want to go, he or she will simply not show up and then will avoid you completely in the future. Instead, try asking, "What are you doing Sunday morning?" If your friend doesn't have any plans, then say, "I would love to have you come and join us for our church service this Sunday or any Sunday you are free. Just let me know." This gives your friend the option of deciding whether he or she wants to go and allows him or her an "out" without actually having to say no.
- Don't denigrate Thai royalty. Many Christians think of the movie *The King and I* when they think of Thailand. Most Thais who see this movie (and the play) consider it an insult to one of their most respected kings. Neither the play nor the movie has been shown in Thailand. Avoid talking about it.
- As with people from most other countries, avoid discussing politics.
- Don't get into discussions about drug trafficking.

## VIETNAM

*Population:* 79.9 million

*Ethnicity:* Vietnamese (85 to 90 percent), Other—including Chinese, Hmong, and Thai (10 to 15 percent)

*Religions/Religious Groups:* Buddhist, Christian—mostly Catholic, Muslim (no official statistics available)

*Languages:* Vietnamese and English; some Chinese, Khmer, and French

*How to Greet the Vietnamese*
- Use titles (such as Dr., Professor, Mr., Mrs., and so on) along with the person's first name (which is actually the family name). Friends use given names.
- Handshakes are common, although men should wait for a woman to offer her hand first. Handshakes are accompanied with a slight bow of the head to indicate respect.

*Speak Vietnamese!*
A strong and immediate bridge can be built with your Vietnamese friend if you know just a few phrases in his or her language. The fact that you took the trouble and made an attempt will mean a lot. You will develop rapport almost immediately and, invariably, evoke a smile. Here are some common phrases in Vietnamese, which are written as they would be pronounced:

Hello: *Sihn chao*
Good-bye: *Tom bee-at*
Good morning/afternoon/evening: *Sihn chao*
Please: *Lahm urn*
Thank you: *Cahm urn*
Yes: *Dah*
No: *Khon*

*Things to Remember When Interacting with the Vietnamese*
- Among the Vietnamese, the family name comes first, followed by the first name.
- In Vietnam there is great respect for the elderly. One's parents and grandparents are shown the utmost respect and honor. Vietnamese people are often shocked at the way older people are treated in America. Showing disrespect to the elderly, sending older members of the family to nursing homes, and openly disagreeing with them are often seen as brutal and cruel acts. Be prepared to discuss this topic if it ever comes up and explain why it is this way in this country.

- If you are invited to a Vietnamese home, it is customary to bring a small gift such as tea or flowers. Avoid red roses because of romantic implications.
- If you eat with chopsticks, be sure to place them on the table on top of the napkin after you are done.
- Vietnamese people tend to talk in a low voice and dislike loud behavior.
- Your Vietnamese friend may ask you personal questions. Be prepared for them.

### Be Aware of These Gestures

- If invited to a Vietnamese home, ask whether you should remove your shoes before entering the house.
- Pointing with the index finger is considered rude.
- Don't point your feet or shoes at your Vietnamese friend.
- Use both hands when receiving or giving things.

### Sensitive Issues

- Avoid questions that may have a negative answer. The Vietnamese dislike saying no. If you invite a Vietnamese friend to a church event, and he or she replies, "Good," you may think that your friend will be there. But if your friend does not really want to go, he or she will simply not show up and then will avoid you completely in the future. Instead, try asking, "What are you doing Sunday morning?" If your friend doesn't have any plans, then say, "I would love to have you come and join us for our church service this Sunday or any Sunday you are free. Just let me know." This gives your friend the option of deciding whether he or she wants to go and allows him or her an "out" without actually having to say no.
- As in most other countries, politics is a sensitive issue—avoid the topic.
- Don't touch the head of a Vietnamese person (not even a child's). The head is considered holy and sacred.

- Don't criticize your Vietnamese friend in front of others; this will cause him or her to lose face (become humiliated).
- Don't say or do anything that might be interpreted as making fun of the altars in Vietnamese homes that are dedicated to the worship of ancestors.

# 9

# Africa

This chapter provides specific information to help you relate to friends and acquaintances from countries in Africa that have the largest numbers of people living in America. For guidelines on interacting with internationals, please review chapter 5, "General Guidelines for Cross-Cultural Interaction."

## ALGERIA

*Population:* 31.7 million
*Ethnicity:* Arab-Berber (99 percent), Other (1 percent)
*Religions/Religious Groups:* Officially Muslim (99 percent), Other (1 percent)
*Languages:* Arabic, French, and Berber dialects

### How to Greet an Algerian
- Use titles (such as Dr., Professor, Mr., Mrs., and so on) along with the last name of the person. Friends use first names.
- Handshakes are common, although men should wait for a woman to offer her hand first.

### Speak Arabic!
A strong and immediate bridge can be built with your Algerian friend if you know just a few phrases of his or her language. The fact that you took the

trouble and made an attempt will mean a lot to your friend. You will develop rapport almost immediately and, invariably, evoke a smile. Many Algerians also speak French. (To learn a few phrases in French, see the section in chapter 7 on France). Here are some common phrases in Arabic, which are written as they would be pronounced:

Hello: *Us-sah-lahm ah-lay-kum* (usually responded to with *Wah-lay-kum sah-lahm*)

Good-bye: *Mah ahs-sah-lah-mah*

Good morning: *Sah-bah al-kair*

Good afternoon/evening: *Mah-sah al-kair*

Good night: *Tis-bah-hee ah-lah kair*

Please: *Min fahd-luck*

Thank you: *Shook-rahn*

Yes: *Nahm*

No: *Lah*

### *Things to Remember When Interacting with an Algerian*

- Algerian culture is highly collectivist. This means that most Algerians will consider their acceptance of the gospel in light of how it will impact their family and friends. Chances are you may not get an immediate response. There is also a strong possibility of being disowned by family members if a person changes his or her religion. So be patient and supportive of your Algerian friend if he or she struggles spiritually.
- Algerians are usually reserved with strangers. However, once they get to know you, they can be much more expressive.
- Most Algerians are Muslims. Review chapter 15 on Islam before trying to witness to an Algerian. Also, Muslims don't eat pork—keep this in mind if you invite an Algerian friend to your house for a meal.
- If you are invited to an Algerian home, it is customary to bring fruit or flowers—although you should bring only odd numbers of flowers

(except one or thirteen). Avoid red roses because of their romantic implications.

### Be Aware of These Gestures
- If your Algerian friend presses his or her hand over the heart, it signifies gratitude or appreciation.
- Pointing with the index finger is considered rude.
- Don't use your left hand when eating or when receiving or giving things. The left hand is considered unclean, so use only your right hand.
- Don't put your feet on a table or on other furniture.
- Don't point your feet or shoes at your Algerian friend.

### Sensitive Issues
- As with people from most other countries, politics is a sensitive issue—avoid the topic.
- Avoid discussions regarding the Israeli-Palestinian conflict.
- Don't criticize your Algerian friend in front of others; this will cause him or her to lose face (become humiliated).
- Avoid discussions about Islamic fundamentalists, terrorism, and so on.
- Never criticize an Algerian man's moustache—this is considered highly insulting.
- Never poke fun at traditional Algerian attire.

## KENYA
*Population:* 30.8 million
*Ethnicity:* Other (28 percent), Kikuyu (22 percent), Luhya (14 percent), Luo (13 percent), Kalenjin (12 percent), Kamba (11 percent)
*Religions/Religious Groups:* Protestant (38 percent), Roman Catholic (28 percent), Indigenous Beliefs (26 percent), Other (8 percent)
*Languages:* English, Swahili, and other indigenous languages

*How to Greet a Kenyan*
- Use titles (such as Dr., Professor, Mr., Mrs., and so on) along with the last name of the person. Your Kenyan friend will soon prefer using first names.
- Handshakes are common.

*Speak Swahili!*

A strong and immediate bridge can be built with your Kenyan friend if you know just a few phrases of Swahili. The fact that you took the trouble and made an attempt will mean a lot. You will develop rapport almost immediately and, invariably, evoke a smile. Here are some common phrases in Swahili:

Hello: *Salama* (sah-lah-mah) or *Jambo* (jum-bo)

See you! *Tutaonana* (too-tao-nah-nah)

Good morning: *Habari za asubuhi* (hah-bah-ree zah ah-su-bu-nee)

Good afternoon: *Habari za mchana* (hah-bah-ree zah um-cha-nah)

Good evening/night: *Habari za jioni* (hah-bah-ree zah jee-o-nee)

How are you? *Habari?* (hah-bah-ree?)

Fine: *Salama* (sah-lah-mah) or *Sijambo* (see-jum-bo)

Please: *Tafadhali* (tah-fah-dah-lee)

Thank you: *Asante* (ah-sahn-teh)

No Problem! *Hakuna Matata!* (hah-koo-nah mah-tah-tah!)

Yes: *Ndiyo* (dee-yo, beginning with a slight nasal sound "n")

No: *Hapana* (hah-pah-nah)

*Things to Remember When Interacting with a Kenyan*
- Kenyan culture is collectivist. This means that most Kenyans will consider their acceptance of the gospel in light of how it will impact their family and friends. Chances are you may not get an immediate response, so be patient and supportive of your Kenyan friend if he or she struggles spiritually.
- Kenyans are very friendly people.
- If invited to a Kenyan home, it is customary to bring tea, coffee, or flowers. Avoid red roses because of their romantic implications.

- Safe topics for conversation include Kenyan culture and heritage. Kenyans are also proud of their wildlife reserves (several million acres of national reserves exist in Kenya). It is also okay to inquire about their family members.

### Be Aware of These Gestures
- Don't use the left hand when eating, shaking hands, or giving and receiving things.
- Pointing with the index finger is considered rude.
- Don't touch an elderly Kenyan—it is considered very improper.

### Sensitive Issues
- As with people of most other countries, politics is a sensitive issue, so avoid the topic.
- Kenyans often have a strong affiliation to their particular tribe—don't lump them together or confuse one tribe with another.
- Avoid talking about poverty in Kenya.
- Don't confuse Kenya with any other African countries.
- Don't make stereotypical assumptions about Kenyans living in huts or forests.
- Never poke fun at traditional Kenyan attire.

## NIGERIA
*Population:* 126.6 million
*Ethnicity:* Many ethnic groups
*Religions/Religious Groups:* Muslim (50 percent), Christian (40 percent), Indigenous Beliefs (10 percent)
*Languages:* English, Hausa, Yoruba, Igbo, and Fulani

### How to Greet a Nigerian
- Use titles and last names. Go on a first-name basis only if first names are initiated by your Nigerian friend.
- Handshakes are common and may be done several times even during a

short meeting. In fact, it may be considered rude if you don't shake hands.

- Don't rush through a greeting; rushing can be considered rude.

## Things to Remember When Interacting with a Nigerian

- Safe topics of conversation include Nigerian culture and sports (soccer and cricket are among the most popular sports).
- Many Nigerians are Muslims. Review chapter 15 on Islam before trying to witness to a Nigerian. Also, Muslims don't eat pork, so keep this in mind if you invite a Nigerian friend to your house for a meal.
- Nigerians are very hospitable and friendly.
- Nigeria, like many other African nations, is divided into several tribes, each with their own customs and traditions. In Nigeria the major tribes include the *Hausa* (consisting of devout Muslims); *Ibo* (more materialistic than the others, practical, and resourceful); and *Yoruba* (friendly and outgoing, love having a good time).
- On the whole, Nigerians tend to be more self-confident than most other African cultures. This means you can expect a vigorous debate about Christianity.
- Don't be surprised if, after hearing the gospel, your Nigerian friend seems convinced but refuses to make a decision. This is often because this person is thinking of his or her family. Families (and extended families) play a very important role in Nigerian society, and an individual may find it hard to accept the gospel if he or she feels this would go against the interests or wishes of the family.
- In Nigeria there is great respect for the elderly. One's parents and grandparents are shown the utmost respect and honor. Nigerians are often shocked at the way older people are treated in America. Showing disrespect to the elderly, sending older members of the family to nursing homes, and openly disagreeing with them are often seen as brutal and cruel acts. Be prepared to discuss this if it ever comes up.

- Don't be surprised if you end up receiving advice and/or criticism from your Nigerian friend. This is normal.
- Nigerians tend to ask personal questions. Be prepared for them.

### Be Aware of These Gestures

- Personal space among Nigerians is smaller than in the United States; when conversing, don't be surprised if your Nigerian friend stands closer than you're accustomed to. Backing away is usually a mistake, as your Nigerian friend will simply step forward to close the gap.
- The thumbs-up sign is sometimes seen as an insult.
- Don't use the left hand when eating, shaking hands, or giving and receiving things.
- Don't point your feet or the soles of your shoes toward a Nigerian.
- When visiting a Nigerian home, keep your hands above the table and not on your lap. However, don't put your elbows on the table.

### Sensitive Issues

- Avoid discussing the tensions between the different ethnic groups of Nigeria.
- As with people from most other countries, avoid discussing politics.
- Don't make stereotypical assumptions about Nigerians living in huts or forests.
- Never make fun of traditional Nigerian attire.

## SOUTH AFRICA

*Population:* 43.6 million

*Ethnicity:* Black (75 percent), White (14 percent), Mixed (9 percent), Other (2 percent)

*Religions/Religious Groups:* Christian (68 percent), Animism and Indigenous Beliefs (28.5 percent), Other (3.5 percent)

*Languages:* A total of eleven official languages including English and Afrikaans

### How to Greet a South African

- Use titles (such as Dr., Professor, Mr., Mrs., and so on) along with the last name of the person. Friends use first names.
- Handshakes are common.

### Things to Remember When Interacting with a South African

- Although South African culture is somewhat individualistic, most South Africans (especially blacks) will probably consider family members before making any final decisions about the gospel. Chances are you may not get an immediate response, so be patient and supportive of your South African friend if he or she wrestles spiritually.
- South Africa has two parallel cultures: individualistic, liberal whites and collectivist, conservative blacks. In recent times considerable progress has been made toward reconciliation among these groups.
- Safe topics for conversation include tourism, sports (cricket is a popular sport), and South Africa's natural beauty.
- Some black South Africans may mix ancestor worship with Christian beliefs.

### Be Aware of These Gestures

- Don't leave your hat on when entering your South African friend's house.
- Pointing with the index finger is considered rude.
- Don't put your hands in your pockets while talking.
- Avoid using your left hand when eating or receiving or giving things. (This is frowned upon more among blacks than among whites.)

*Sensitive Issues*
- As with people from most other countries, avoid discussing politics.
- Don't discuss South Africa's history of apartheid.

## ZIMBABWE

*Population:* 11.4 million

*Ethnicity:* Shona (71 percent), Ndebele (16 percent), Other (13 percent)

*Religions/Religious Groups:* Syncretism (50 percent—mixing Christian and animistic beliefs), Christian (25 percent), Indigenous Beliefs (24 percent), Other (1 percent)

*Languages:* English, Shona, Sindebele, and several other tribal dialects

*How to Greet a Zimbabwean*
- Use titles (such as Dr., Professor, Mr., Mrs., and so on) along with the last name of the person. Friends use first names.
- Handshakes are common.

*Things to Remember When Interacting with a Zimbabwean*
- Zimbabwean culture is collectivist. This means that most Zimbabweans will consider their acceptance of the gospel in light of how it will impact their family and friends. Chances are you may not get an immediate response, so be patient and support your Zimbabwean friend if he or she struggles spiritually.
- Zimbabweans are friendly and polite.
- Keep in mind that although many Zimbabweans claim to be Christians, they also practice spiritualism and witchcraft.
- In Zimbabwe there is great respect for the elderly. One's parents and grandparents are shown the utmost respect and honor. Zimbabweans are often shocked at the way older people are treated in the United States. Showing disrespect to the elderly, sending older members of the family to nursing homes, and openly disagreeing with them are often seen as brutal and cruel acts. Be prepared to discuss this topic if it ever comes up.

## Be Aware of These Gestures
- Use both hands when receiving or giving things.
- Zimbabweans often clap to signify gratitude.
- Staring is considered rude.

## Sensitive Issues
- As with people from most other countries, politics is a sensitive issue, so avoid the topic.
- Don't criticize your Zimbabwean friend in front of others, as this will cause him or her to lose face (become humiliated).
- Avoid discussing racial issues.

# 10

# The Middle East

This chapter provides specific information to help you relate to friends and acquaintances from Middle Eastern countries. For guidelines on interacting with internationals, please review chapter 5, "General Guidelines for Cross-Cultural Interaction."

### EGYPT
*Population:* 69.5 million

*Ethnicity:* Egyptian, Bedouin, Berber (99 percent—Eastern Hamitic stock), Other (1 percent)

*Religions/Religious Groups:* Muslim (94 percent), Other—including Coptic Christian (6 percent)

*Languages:* Arabic, English, and French

### How to Greet an Egyptian
- Use titles (such as Dr., Professor, Mr., Mrs., and so on) along with the last name of the person. Friends use first names.
- Handshakes are common, although men should wait for a woman to offer her hand first.
- See the section on Algeria to learn a few phrases in Arabic. This will help create rapport with your Egyptian friend.

*Things to Remember When Interacting with an Egyptian*

- Egyptian culture is highly collectivist. This means that most Egyptians will consider their acceptance of the gospel in light of how it will impact their family and friends. Chances are you may not get an immediate response. There is also a strong possibility of an Egyptian being disowned by family members if he or she changes religions. So be patient and support your Egyptian friend if he or she struggles spiritually.

- Egyptians tend to be very expressive, both verbally and nonverbally.

- If you are invited to an Egyptian home, don't be surprised if your host or hostess welcomes you several times. It is okay to bring cake or chocolates. Also, remember Egyptians are highly generous people. Be careful not to praise an object too much, or you may end up taking it home with you!

- Safe topics of conversation include Egyptian culture and history. Sports (especially soccer and tennis) is a popular and good topic to talk about.

- Religion is a volatile topic, so wait until you get to know your Egyptian friend before talking about your faith in God.

- Be prepared to build a relationship and share the gospel over a period of time. An Egyptian will be more open to hearing what you have to say once he or she trusts you, and trust can only be built over many weeks and months.

- Most Egyptians are Muslims. Read chapter 15 on Islam before trying to witness to an Egyptian. Also, Muslims don't eat pork, so keep this in mind if you invite an Egyptian friend to your house for a meal.

- If you are invited to an Egyptian home for a meal, always leave a little bit of food on the plate. This means you enjoyed the meal and that you are satisfied. Some Egyptians consider it an insult if you add salt to your food.

- If you invite an Egyptian friend over for a meal, rice, bread, vegetables, and chicken are popular dishes.

*Be Aware of These Gestures*
- Personal space among Egyptians is smaller than in the United States. When conversing, don't be surprised if your Egyptian friend stands closer than you're accustomed to. Backing away is usually a mistake, as your Egyptian friend will simply step forward to close the gap.
- The left hand is considered unclean, so avoid using it when eating, shaking hands, or giving and receiving things.
- If you are invited to an Egyptian home, ask whether you should remove your shoes before entering the house.
- Don't point your feet or the soles of your shoes toward an Egyptian.
- Don't put your feet on a table or on other furniture.
- Pointing with the index finger is considered rude.
- The thumbs-up gesture is considered rude and offensive.

*Sensitive Issues*
- Avoid talking about politics or the Israeli-Palestinian conflict. However, you may find your Egyptian friend quite eager to discuss it; in that case, be sure to do more listening than talking.
- Reputation and honor are considered among the highest values. For this reason, don't criticize your Egyptian friend or his or her beliefs in front of others. This may cause your friend to lose face (become humiliated).
- Stay away from discussions on Islamic extremists (a minority in Egypt) and their role in terrorism.

# IRAN
*Population:* 66.1 million
*Ethnicity:* Persian (51 percent), Other (25 percent), Azeri (24 percent)
*Religions/Religious Groups:* Muslim (99 percent), Christian, Jewish, Baha'i, and Zoroastrian (1 percent)
*Languages:* Persian, Persian dialects, Turkic, Kurdish, Luri, Balochi, and Arabic

## *How to Greet an Iranian*

- Use titles (such as Dr., Professor, Mr., Mrs., and so on) along with the last name of the person. Friends use first names.
- Handshakes are common, although men should wait for a woman to offer her hand first. In traditional Iranian families, it is considered inappropriate for women to shake hands with men. However, it is okay to shake hands with children.

## *Things to Remember When Interacting with an Iranian*

- Iranian culture is highly collectivist. This means that most Iranians will consider their acceptance of the gospel in light of how it will impact their family and friends. Chances are you may not get an immediate response. There is also a strong possibility that an Iranian will be disowned by family members if he or she changes religions. So be patient and support your Iranian friend if he or she struggles spiritually.
- Most Iranians are Muslims. Read chapter 15 on Islam before trying to share the gospel with an Iranian. Also, Muslims don't eat pork, so keep this in mind if you invite an Iranian friend to your house for a meal.
- Safe topics for conversation include Iranian culture, hobbies, children, and education.
- Religion is a volatile topic, so wait until you get to know your Iranian friend before sharing the gospel.
- Be prepared to build a relationship over a period of time. Iranians will be more open to hearing what you have to say once they trust you, and trust can only be built over many weeks and months.
- If you are invited to an Iranian home, it is customary to bring candy or flowers. Avoid red roses because of romantic implications. Also, be careful not to praise an object too much, or your friend may give it to you!

## *Be Aware of These Gestures*

- If invited to an Iranian home, ask whether you should take off your shoes before entering the house.

- Sometimes an Iranian may shake his or her head side to side to indicate understanding or affirmation—or up and down to indicate a negative answer (exactly the opposite of how these gestures are viewed in America).
- Pointing with the index finger is considered rude.
- The thumbs-up sign is considered an obscene gesture.
- The left hand is considered unclean, so avoid using it when eating, shaking hands, or giving and receiving things.
- Don't point your feet or the soles of your shoes toward an Iranian.

### Sensitive Issues

- As with people of most other cultures, politics is a sensitive issue— avoid the topic.
- Avoid talking about the Israeli-Palestinian conflict.
- Reputation and honor are considered among the highest values. For this reason, don't criticize your Iranian friend or his or her beliefs in front of others. This may cause him or her to lose face (become humiliated).
- Contrary to popular belief, most Iranians like Westerners and admire our advancements in many spheres. However, many view Western culture as degenerative. Don't compare Iran to the United States.
- Don't initiate any conversation on the Iraqi-Iranian conflict.
- Avoid discussions about terrorism, the 1979 U.S. embassy hostage crisis, and the Ayatollah Khomeini.

## IRAQ

*Population:* 23.3 million

*Ethnicity:* Arab (75 to 80 percent), Kurdish (15 to 20 percent), Assyrian and Turkoman (1 to 5 percent)

*Religions/Religious Groups:* Muslim (97 percent), Other—including Christian (3 percent)

*Languages:* Arabic, Kurdish (official in Kurdish regions), Assyrian, and Armenian

### How to Greet an Iraqi

- Use titles (such as Dr., Professor, Mr., Mrs., and so on) along with the last name of the person. Friends use first names.
- Handshakes are common, although men should wait for a woman to offer her hand first. In traditional Iraqi families, it is considered inappropriate for women to shake hands with men. It is okay to shake hands with children.
- See the section on Algeria to learn a few phrases in Arabic. This will help create rapport with your Iraqi friend.

### Things to Remember When Interacting with an Iraqi

- Iraqi culture is highly collectivist. This means that most Iraqis will consider their acceptance of the gospel in light of how it will impact their family and friends. Chances are you may not receive an immediate response. There is also a strong possibility that your Iraqi friend will be disowned by family members if he or she changes religions. So be patient and support your Iraqi friend if he or she struggles spiritually.
- Most Iraqis are Muslims. Read chapter 15 on Islam before trying to witness to an Iraqi. Also, Muslims don't eat pork, so keep this in mind if you invite an Iraqi friend to your house for a meal.
- Although most Iraqis are Muslims, a small percentage of the population are Chaldeans. Chaldeans are Catholics and have fled Iraq in large numbers for many years. Hence, you are as likely to come across an Iraqi Chaldean as an Iraqi Muslim in North America. Don't confuse the two, as there are deep-seated hostilities between the two groups. Encourage your Chaldean friend to seek a deeper relationship with Christ.
- Religion is a volatile topic, so wait until you get to know your Iraqi friend before sharing the gospel.
- Safe topics for conversation include Iraqi culture, hobbies, children, and education.
- Be prepared to build a relationship and talk about Christ over a period of time. Iraqis will be more open to hearing what you have to

say once they trust you, and trust can only be built over many weeks and months.

### Be Aware of These Gestures

- If invited to an Iraqi home, ask whether you should remove your shoes before entering the house.
- Pointing with the index finger is considered rude.
- The left hand is considered unclean, so avoid using it when eating, shaking hands, or giving and receiving things.
- Don't point your feet or the soles of your shoes toward an Iraqi.

### Sensitive Issues

- As elsewhere, politics is a sensitive issue—avoid the topic.
- Avoid talking about the Israeli-Palestinian conflict.
- Reputation and honor are considered among the highest values. For this reason, don't criticize your Iraqi friend or his or her beliefs in front of others. This may cause your friend to lose face (become humiliated).
- Don't initiate any conversation about the Iraqi-Iranian conflict.
- Avoid discussions on terrorism, the Gulf War, or the recent U.S.-led overthrow of Saddam Hussein's regime.
- Many Iraqis living in this country will tell you that they see the conflict between Iraq and the United States as a conflict between two governments, not between two people groups. For this reason, many of them are eager to get to know Americans. However, it is important to note that there are some Iraqis who still harbor strong affiliation with their home country and don't view U.S. policies favorably. They are harder to relate to and often will not even consider building a relationship with an American. Pray for God's guidance.

## ISRAEL

*Population:* 5.9 million

*Ethnicity:* Jewish (80 percent), non-Jewish (20 percent—mostly Arab)

*Religions/Religious Groups:* Jewish (80 percent), Muslim (15 percent), Other
(5 percent)
*Languages:* Hebrew (official), Arabic, and English

### How to Greet an Israeli
- This is one country in which almost everyone uses first names.
- Handshakes are common. Close friends pat each other on the shoulders.

### Speak Hebrew!
A strong bridge can be built with your Israeli friend if you know just a few
phrases in his or her language. The fact that you took the trouble and made an
attempt will mean a lot. You will develop rapport almost immediately and,
invariably, evoke a smile. Here are some common phrases in Hebrew, which are
written as they would be pronounced:

Hello: *Sha-lohm*
Good-bye: *Sha-lohm*
Good morning: *Bo-ker tov*
Good evening: *Brev tov*
How are you? *Mah shlo-mehk?*
Fine: *Meht-su-yahn*
Please: *Bay-vah-kah-shah*
Thank you: *Toh-dah*
Yes: *Ken*
No: *Lo*

### Things to Remember When Interacting with an Israeli
- Although Israeli culture is somewhat individualistic, most Israelis will
  probably consider family members before making any final decisions
  about the gospel. Chances are you may not receive an immediate
  response, so be patient and supportive of your Israeli friend if he or she
  struggles spiritually.
- A popular topic of conversation involves family matters.

- Soccer is a very popular sport in Israel.
- Keep in mind that Israelis enjoy frank discussions. If the topic of religion comes up, your Israeli friends will probably let you know exactly how they feel. Be prepared to talk about God in the context of pain and suffering.
- Since more than 80 percent of Israelis are Jews, study chapter 16 on Judaism before witnessing to an Israeli.
- If you are invited to an Israeli home, it is customary to bring chocolates or flowers, but avoid red roses because of romantic implications. Also, leave a little bit of food on your plate to signify that you are satisfied. If you don't, your host will think you are still hungry.
- Most Israelis don't eat pork or ham for religious reasons.

### Be Aware of These Gestures
- Israelis tend to have a smaller personal space than Americans do. When conversing, don't be surprised if your Israeli friend stands closer than you're accustomed to. Backing away is usually a mistake, as your Israeli friend will simply step forward to close the gap.
- The left hand is considered unclean, so use only your right hand when eating, shaking hands, giving or receiving things.
- The thumbs-up gesture is considered rude and offensive.

### Sensitive Issues
- Although Israelis love talking about politics (and certainly the Middle East situation), avoid being drawn into such conversations. Do more listening than talking.

## JORDAN
*Population:* 5.1 million
*Ethnicity:* Arab (98 percent), Other (2 percent)
*Religions/Religious Groups:* Muslim (96 percent), Christian (4 percent)
*Languages:* Arabic (official) and English

## *How to Greet a Jordanian*

- Use titles (such as Dr., Professor, Mr., Mrs., and so on) along with the last name of the person. Friends use first names.
- Handshakes are common, although men should wait for a woman to offer her hand first.
- See the section on Algeria to learn a few phrases in Arabic. This will help create rapport with your Jordanian friend.

## *Things to Remember When Interacting with a Jordanian*

- Jordanian culture is highly collectivist. This means that most Jordanians will consider their acceptance of the gospel in light of how it will impact their family and friends. Chances are you may not get an immediate response. There is also a strong possibility that a Jordanian will be disowned by family members if he or she changes religions. So be patient and support your Jordanian friend if he or she struggles spiritually.
- Jordanians are friendly people.
- Safe topics of conversation include Jordanian culture, hobbies, and sports.
- Most Jordanians are Muslims. Read chapter 15 on Islam before trying to witness to a Jordanian. Also, Muslims don't eat pork, so keep this in mind if you invite a Jordanian friend to your house for a meal.

## *Be Aware of These Gestures*

- If invited to a Jordanian home, ask whether you should remove your shoes before entering the house.
- The left hand is considered unclean, so avoid using it when eating, shaking hands, or giving and receiving things.
- Don't point your feet or the soles of your shoes toward a Jordanian.
- Don't rub the back of your hand on your forehead—it is considered a sign of disrespect.
- If you are invited to a Jordanian home, it is customary to bring fruit or flowers. Avoid red roses because of their romantic implications.

- Before you begin eating, wait until everyone is seated and a blessing is said. If your host is Muslim, an Islamic prayer will be offered before anyone eats.
- After a meal, leave a little bit of food on your plate to signify that you are satisfied. If you don't, your host will think you are still hungry.

### Sensitive Issues

- Avoid talking about politics or the Israeli-Palestinian conflict.
- Reputation and honor are considered among the highest values. For this reason, don't criticize your Jordanian friend or his or her beliefs in front of others. This may cause him or her to lose face (become humiliated).

## SAUDI ARABIA

*Population:* 22.8 million
*Ethnicity:* Arab (90 percent), Afro-Asian (10 percent)
*Religions/Religious Groups:* Muslim (100 percent)
*Languages:* Arabic

### How to Greet a Saudi

- Use titles (such as Dr., Professor, Mr., Mrs., and so on) along with the last name of the person. Friends use first names.
- Handshakes are common, although men should wait for a woman to offer her hand first. In traditional Saudi families, it is considered inappropriate for women to shake hands with men.
- See the section on Algeria to learn a few phrases in Arabic. This will help create rapport with your Saudi friend.

### Things to Remember When Interacting with a Saudi

- Saudi culture is highly collectivist. This means that most Saudis will consider their acceptance of the gospel in light of how it will impact their family and friends. Chances are you may not receive an immediate response. There is also a strong possibility that a Saudi will be disowned by family members if he or she changes religions. So be patient and support your Saudi friend if he or she struggles spiritually.

- Saudi history, sports, and horse and camel racing are safe topics of conversation.
- If you see two Saudis talking loudly to each other, don't be alarmed. They may simply be discussing household affairs.
- As almost all Saudis are Muslims, read chapter 15 on Islam before trying to witness to your Saudi friend. Also, Muslims don't eat pork, so keep this in mind if you invite a Saudi friend to your house for a meal.
- Religion is a volatile topic, so wait until you get to know your Saudi friend before sharing the gospel.
- Be prepared to build a relationship and talk about Christ over a period of time. Saudis will be more open to hearing what you have to say once they trust you, and trust can only be built over many weeks and months.
- Saudis generally don't talk while eating.

### Be Aware of These Gestures

- Personal space is much smaller in Saudi Arabia than in the United States. When conversing, don't be surprised if your Saudi friend stands very close to you, touches you, and leans over to you frequently. This occurs, of course, between members of the same gender.
- If invited to the home of a Saudi, ask whether you should remove your shoes before entering the house.
- Don't point your finger.
- Don't point the bottom of your feet or your shoes to a Saudi.
- The left hand is considered unclean, so avoid using it when eating, shaking hands, or giving and receiving things.
- The thumbs-up gesture is considered rude and offensive.

### Sensitive Issues

- Avoid talking about politics or the Israeli-Palestinian conflict.
- Avoid discussing the role of women under Islam or in Saudi Arabia.

- Reputation and honor are considered among the highest values. For this reason, don't criticize your Saudi friend or his or her beliefs in front of others. This may cause him or her to lose face (become humiliated).

## SYRIA
*Population:* 16.7 million
*Ethnicity:* Arab (90 percent), Other (10 percent)
*Religions/Religious Groups:* Muslim (90 percent), Christian (10 percent)
*Languages:* Arabic (official), Kurdish, Aramaic, and Armenian

### How to Greet a Syrian
- Use titles (such as Dr., Professor, Mr., Mrs., and so on) along with the last name of the person. Friends use first names.
- Handshakes are common, although men should wait for a woman to offer her hand first. In traditional Syrian families, it is considered inappropriate for women to shake hands with men.
- See the section on Algeria to learn a few phrases in Arabic. This will help create rapport with your Syrian friend.

### Things to Remember When Interacting with a Syrian
- Syrian culture is highly collectivist. This means that most Syrians will consider their acceptance of the gospel in light of how it will impact their family and friends. Chances are you may not get an immediate response. There is also a strong possibility that a Syrian will be disowned by family members if he or she changes religions. So be patient and support your Syrian friend if he or she struggles spiritually.
- Most Syrians are Muslims. Read chapter 15 on Islam before trying to witness to a Syrian. Also, Muslims don't eat pork, so keep this in mind if you invite a Syrian friend to your house for a meal.

### Be Aware of These Gestures
- If invited to a Syrian home, ask whether you should remove your shoes before entering the house.

- Pointing with the index finger is considered rude.
- The left hand is regarded as unclean, so avoid using it when eating, shaking hands, or giving and receiving things.
- Don't point your feet or the soles of your shoes toward a Syrian.

### Sensitive Issues

- Avoid talking about politics or the Israeli-Palestinian conflict.
- Reputation and honor are considered among the highest values. For this reason, don't criticize your Syrian friend or his or her beliefs in front of others. This may cause your friend to lose face (become humiliated).
- Contrary to what some may believe, most Syrians like Americans and admire our advancements in many spheres. However, many view Western culture as degenerate. Syrian culture promotes high moral values, and they see American society as having low morals.
- Don't compare Syria to the United States.
- Stay away from discussions about terrorism and Islamic extremists in Syria.

# 11

# Latin America

This chapter provides specific information to help you relate to friends and acquaintances from Latin American countries. For guidelines on interacting with internationals, please review chapter 5, "General Guidelines for Cross-Cultural Interaction."

## ARGENTINA

*Population:* 37.4 million

*Ethnicity:* White (85 percent—Spanish and Italian for the most part), Non-white (15 percent—including Mestizo and Amerindian)

*Religions/Religious Groups:* Nominal Catholics (90 percent), Other (10 percent)

*Languages:* Spanish (official), English, Italian, German, and French

### How to Greet an Argentine

- A handshake and a slight nod are appropriate. Men should wait for a woman to offer her hand first.
- A common greeting is *"Buenos días"* (pronounced bwey-nohs dee-ahs), which means "Good day."
- An *abrazo,* consisting of a hug, handshake, and several thumps on the shoulder, is usually reserved for close friends.

- Referring to Argentines by title is surprisingly pleasant to them, since it is the custom back home. Refer to them as Señor (Mr.), Señora (Mrs.), or Señorita (Miss) followed by their last name.
- See the section on Spain to learn a few phrases of Spanish. This will help create quick rapport with your Argentine friend.

## Things to Remember When Interacting with an Argentine

- Argentine culture is collectivist. This means that most Argentines will consider their acceptance of the gospel in light of how it will impact their family and friends. Chances are you may not receive an immediate response, so be patient and support your Argentine friend if he or she struggles spiritually.
- Argentines are great fans of soccer (called *fútbol* [foot-bole] in Argentina), so sports are a great topic for conversation. So are fine arts, food, sightseeing, and children.
- Most Argentines love beef (they lead the world in per capita beef consumption).
- Argentines, like other Latin Americans, are very social and friendly.
- Argentines like being complimented about their children.
- If you are invited to an Argentine home, it is customary to bring chocolates or flowers for your hosts. Avoid red roses because of their romantic implications.
- Your Argentine friend may ask you personal questions, so be prepared for them.

## Be Aware of These Gestures

- Argentines have a smaller personal space than Americans. When conversing, don't be surprised if an Argentine stands very close to you. Backing up is usually a mistake, as your Argentine friend will simply step forward to close the gap.
- Friends often pat each other on the back.
- Yawning without covering your mouth is considered rude.

- When visiting an Argentine home, keep your hands above the table and not on your lap. However, don't put your elbows on the table.
- Maintain eye contact, but don't stare.
- Pointing with the index finger is considered rude.
- Propping your leg on a table is seen as impolite.
- The thumbs-up sign is regarded as an offensive gesture.

### Sensitive Issues
- Avoid discussing politics—especially Argentine politics.
- Religion is a sensitive issue with many Argentines. Of course, you should always be ready to share the gospel at the prompting of the Holy Spirit, but broach this topic only after you get to know your Argentine friend.
- Avoid comparing Argentina with other neighboring Latin American countries (especially Chile) or with the United States, as this is considered inappropriate.

### BRAZIL

*Population:* 174.5 million

*Ethnicity:* White (55 percent), mixed White and Black (38 percent), Black (6 percent), Other (1 percent)

*Religions/Religious Groups:* Roman Catholic (70 percent), Other (30 percent)

*Languages:* Portuguese (official), Spanish, English, and French

### How to Greet a Brazilian
- You are probably safe using first names of Brazilians, but start by using titles and last names. Your Brazilian friend will soon encourage you to switch to a first-name basis.
- Handshakes are common.
- A common form of greeting is *"Come vai?"* which means "How are you?"

*Speak Portuguese!*

A strong and immediate bridge can be built with your Brazilian friend if you know just a few phrases in his or her language. The fact that you took the trouble and made an attempt will mean a lot. You will develop rapport almost immediately and, invariably, evoke a smile. Here are some common phrases in Portuguese:

Good morning: *Bom dia* (bong deer)

Good afternoon: *Boa tarde* (bo-ar taar-der)

Good night: *Boa noite* (bo-ar noy-ter)

Good-bye: *Adeus* (ah-daus)

Please: *Por favor* (poor fer-vo-ar)

Thank you: *Obrigado* (oab-rig-ga-doo)

Yes: *Sim* (sing)

No: *Nao* (naang)

*Things to Remember When Interacting with a Brazilian*

- Brazil, the largest country in South America, is culturally and linguistically different from the rest of the Latin American countries. Brazilians speak Portuguese, while all other Latin American countries speak Spanish. Some Brazilians don't like being called Latino or even Hispanic, as that term literally means "Spanish-speaking."

- Brazilian culture is collectivist. This means that most Brazilians will consider their acceptance of the gospel in light of how it will impact their family and friends. Chances are you may not receive an immediate response, so be patient and supportive of your Brazilian friend if he or she struggles spiritually.

- Brazilians tend to be outgoing and friendly. This makes it easier to bring religion into discussions. Keep in mind that more than 80 percent of Brazilians are nominally Catholic. Share how Christ has made a difference in your life emotionally, spiritually, and practically.

- You might find your Brazilian friend quite boisterous when expressing his or her views. This is normal; Brazilians pride themselves on being passionate people. However, the moment you sense your Brazilian

friend becoming annoyed or irritated, drop the topic. You can pick it up later.
- Safe topics of conversation include Brazilian natural beauty, industry, and sports. Soccer is a very popular sport.
- If you are invited to a Brazilian home, it is customary to bring a gift such as candy.
- Never pick up any food with your fingers, as some Brazilians consider this behavior rude.

### Be Aware of These Gestures
- Personal space among Brazilians is much smaller than in the United States. When conversing, don't be surprised if your Brazilian friend stands closer than you're accustomed to. Backing away is usually a mistake, as your Brazilian friend will simply step forward to close the gap.
- The sign for "okay" or "all right" (using the thumb and forefinger to make a circle) is seen as an indignity.
- Chewing gum while talking is regarded as rude.
- Maintain eye contact, but don't stare.

### Sensitive Issues
- As with people from most other countries, avoid discussing politics.
- Don't get into environmental issues, such as the depletion of rain forests.
- Avoid comparing Brazil with other Latin American countries (especially Argentina) or with the United States.
- Avoid calling a Brazilian a Hispanic or Latino.
- Don't initiate discussions about personal issues.

## CHILE
*Population:* 15.3 million
*Ethnicity:* White and White Amerindian (95 percent), Other (5 percent)

*Religions/Religious Groups:* Roman Catholic (89 percent), Protestant
(11 percent)
*Language:* Spanish

### How to Greet a Chilean

- Use titles (such as Dr., Professor, Mr., Mrs., and so on) along with the last name of the person. Refer to them as Señor (Mr.), Señora (Mrs.), or Señorita (Miss), followed by their last name. Friends use first names.
- Handshakes are common, although men should wait for a woman to offer her hand first.
- See the section on Spain to learn a few phrases in Spanish. This will help create rapport with your Chilean friend.

### Things to Remember When Interacting with a Chilean

- Chilean culture is collectivist. This means that most Chileans will consider their acceptance of the gospel in light of how it will impact their family and friends. Chances are you may not get an immediate response, so be patient and supportive of your Chilean friend if he or she struggles spiritually.
- There are strong Chilean communities in California (mostly in the Los Angeles and San Francisco areas), Boston, New York, Baltimore, New Orleans, Miami, Las Vegas, and Seattle. In 1996 there were some seventy-three thousand people of Chilean origin in the United States. That number has most likely increased since then.
- Sports, Chilean history, fine arts, food, family, and literature are considered safe topics of conversation.
- Chileans are highly patriotic, so talking about Chilean culture and heritage is always a good idea.
- Don't be surprised if your friend constantly interrupts you during conversation. This is considered normal.
- If you are invited to a Chilean home, it is customary to bring candy or flowers. Avoid red roses because of their romantic implications.

*Be Aware of These Gestures*
- Personal space among Chileans is smaller than in the United States. When conversing, don't be surprised if your Chilean friend stands closer than you're accustomed to. Backing away is usually a mistake, as your Chilean friend will simply step forward to close the gap.
- Yawning without covering the mouth is considered rude.
- When visiting a Chilean home, keep your hands above the table and not on your lap. However, don't put your elbows on the table.
- Don't raise a clenched fist over your head—it is considered a communist gesture.
- Pointing with the index finger is considered rude.
- Maintain eye contact, but don't stare.

*Sensitive Issues*
- As with people from most other countries, politics is a sensitive issue, so avoid the topic.
- Don't criticize your Chilean friend in front of others, as this will cause him or her to lose face (become humiliated).
- Don't criticize anything Chilean, since Chileans are known to be strongly patriotic.
- Avoid talking about Chile's relationship with surrounding Latin American nations.

## COLOMBIA
*Population:* 40.3 million
*Ethnicity:* Mestizo (58 percent), White (20 percent), Mulatto (14 percent), Black (4 percent), Other (4 percent)
*Religions/Religious Groups:* Roman Catholic (95 percent), Other (5 percent)
*Language:* Spanish

*How to Greet a Colombian*
- Use titles (such as Dr., Professor, Mr., Mrs., and so on) along with the last name of the person. Refer to them as Señor (Mr.), Señora

(Mrs.), or Señorita (Miss), followed by their last name. Friends use first names.

- Handshakes are common.
- A common phrase for greeting is *"Buenos días"* (pronounced bwey-nohs dee-ahs), which means "Good day."
- An *abrazo,* consisting of a hug, handshake, and several thumps on the shoulder, is usually reserved for close friends.
- See the section on Spain to learn a few phrases in Spanish. This will help create rapport with your Colombian friend.

### Things to Remember When Interacting with a Colombian

- Colombian culture is collectivist. This means that most Colombians will consider their acceptance of the gospel in light of how it will impact their family and friends. Chances are you may not receive an immediate response, so be patient and supportive of your Colombian friend if he or she struggles spiritually.
- Colombians in America are better educated, hold more white-collar jobs, and have a higher median household income than Hispanics as a whole.
- Colombian history, natural beauty, coffee, and art are all safe topics of conversation.
- Sports, especially soccer and bullfights, are other popular topics among Colombians. (See the Sensitive Issues section regarding bullfighting.)
- If you are invited to a Colombian home, it is customary to bring chocolates, nuts, fruit, or flowers. Avoid red roses (because of their romantic implications), marigolds, or lilies (these are associated with funerals).
- After a meal, leave a little bit of food on your plate to signify that you are satisfied. If you don't, your host will think you are still hungry.
- Colombians love stews and soups.
- Avoid questions that may have no as an answer. Colombians dislike confrontations.

### Be Aware of These Gestures

- Personal space among Colombians is smaller than in the United States. When conversing, don't be surprised if your Colombian friend stands closer than you're accustomed to. Backing away is usually a mistake, as your Colombian friend will simply step forward to close the gap.
- Yawning in public is considered rude. If you must yawn, cover your mouth when doing so.
- Don't put your feet on a table or on other furniture.
- Pointing with the index finger is considered rude.
- Maintain eye contact, but don't stare.

### Sensitive Issues

- As with people from most other countries, avoid discussing politics.
- Avoid initiating conversations about the illegal drug trade, kidnappings, and terrorism.
- Similar to dealing with Spaniards, one mistake American Christians (especially those who feel strongly about animal rights) make is to be highly critical of bullfighting. To a Colombian, bullfighting is a sport. Avoid getting into the topic.
- Don't compare Colombia with the United States.
- Don't criticize your Colombian friend in front of others, as this will cause him or her to lose face (become humiliated).

## Costa Rica

*Population:* 3.8 million
*Ethnicity:* White, including Mestizo (96 percent), Other—including Black and Amerindian (4 percent)
*Religions/Religious Groups:* Roman Catholic (95 percent), Other (5 percent)
*Language:* Spanish

### How to Greet a Costa Rican

- Use titles (such as Dr., Professor, Mr., Mrs., and so on) along with the last name of the person. Refer to them as Señor (Mr.), Señora

(Mrs.), or Señorita (Miss), followed by their last name. Friends use first names.

- Handshakes are common, although men should wait for a woman to offer her hand first. Costa Ricans typically give a two-handed handshake.
- See the section on Spain to learn a few phrases in Spanish. This will help create rapport with your Costa Rican friend.

### Things to Remember When Interacting with a Costa Rican

- Costa Rican culture is collectivist. This means that most Costa Ricans will consider their acceptance of the gospel in light of how it will impact their family and friends. Chances are you may not get an immediate response, so be patient and supportive of your Costa Rican friend if he or she struggles spiritually.
- Safe topics for conversation include sports, children, and families.
- If you are invited to a Costa Rican home, it is customary to bring chocolates or flowers. Avoid red roses because of their romantic implications, and lilies, which are used in funerals.
- After a meal, leave a little bit of food on your plate to signify that you are satisfied. If you don't, your host will think you are still hungry.

### Be Aware of These Gestures

- Don't put your feet on a table or on other furniture.
- Always cover your mouth when yawning.
- Chewing gum while talking is seen as rude.
- When visiting a Costa Rican home for a meal, keep your hands above the table and not on your lap. However, don't put your elbows on the table.
- Maintain eye contact, but don't stare.

### Sensitive Issues

- As with people from most other countries, politics is a sensitive issue, so avoid raising the topic. However, keep in mind that Costa Ricans love talking about politics, so if your friend raises the topic, do more listening than talking.

- Don't criticize your Costa Rican friend in front of others; this will cause him or her to lose face (become humiliated).
- Don't ask personal questions.
- Don't refer to your Costa Rican friend as a *"Rican"*—this is considered offensive. Costa Ricans often refer to themselves as *"ticos"* (tee-cohs).

## El Salvador

*Population:* 6.2 million
*Ethnicity:* Mestizo (94 percent), Amerindian (5 percent), Other (1 percent)
*Religions/Religious Groups:* Roman Catholic (75 percent), Other (25 percent)
*Languages:* Spanish and Nahua

### How to Greet a Salvadoran

- Use titles (such as Dr., Professor, Mr., Mrs., and so on) along with the last name of the person. Refer to them as Señor (Mr.), Señora (Mrs.), or Señorita (Miss), followed by their last name. Friends use first names.
- Handshakes are common.
- See the section on Spain to learn a few phrases in Spanish. This will help create rapport with your Salvadoran friend.

### Things to Remember When Interacting with a Salvadoran

- Salvadoran culture is collectivist. This means that most Salvadorans will consider their acceptance of the gospel in light of how it will impact their family and friends. Chances are you may not receive an immediate response, so be patient and supportive of your Salvadoran friend if he or she struggles spiritually.
- Salvadorans usually talk more slowly and softly than Americans do. Don't rush your conversations.
- Safe topics for conversation include family, work, and sports.
- If you are invited to a Salvadoran home, it is customary to bring candy or flowers. Avoid red roses because of their romantic implications, or white flowers, which are used in funerals.
- Don't leave food on your plate, as this is considered rude.

## Be Aware of These Gestures

- Personal space among Salvadorans is smaller than in the United States. When conversing, don't be surprised if your Salvadoran friend stands closer than you're accustomed to. Backing away is usually a mistake, as your Salvadoran friend will simply step forward to close the gap.
- Pointing with the index finger is considered rude.
- Don't point your feet or the soles of your shoes at a Salvadoran.

## Sensitive Issues

- As with people from most other countries, politics is a sensitive issue, so avoid the topic.
- Don't initiate discussions on the Salvadoran civil war. This thirteen-year war, which lasted till 1992, left a fear of uniformed officials among many Salvadorans. This is evident among a number of Salvadorans in the United States.

## GUATEMALA

*Population:* 13 million

*Ethnicity:* Mestizo (56 percent), Amerindian (44 percent)

*Religions/Religious Groups:* Mostly Roman Catholic; also Protestant and Mayan (no official statistics available)

*Languages:* Spanish and Amerindian

## How to Greet a Guatemalan

- Use titles (such as Dr., Professor, Mr., Mrs., and so on) along with the last name of the person. Refer to them as Señor (Mr.), Señora (Mrs.), or Señorita (Miss), followed by their last name. Friends use first names.
- Handshakes are common, although men should wait for a woman to offer her hand first.
- See the section on Spain to learn a few phrases in Spanish. This will help create rapport with your Guatemalan friend.

*Things to Remember When Interacting with a Guatemalan*

- Guatemalan culture is collectivist. This means that most Guatemalans will consider their acceptance of the gospel in light of how it will impact their family and friends. Chances are you may not receive an immediate response, so be patient and supportive of your Guatemalan friend if he or she struggles spiritually.
- If you are invited to a Guatemalan home, it is customary to bring chocolates or flowers. Avoid red roses because of their romantic implications, or white flowers, which are used in funerals.
- If dining in a Guatemalan home, remember that leaving food on your plate is considered rude.
- Safe topics for conversation include Guatemalan culture, history, family, work, hobbies, and sports.
- Your Guatemalan friend may ask you personal questions. Be prepared for them.

*Be Aware of These Gestures*

- Personal space among Guatemalans is smaller than in the United States. When conversing, don't be surprised if your Guatemalan friend stands closer than you're accustomed to. Backing away is usually a mistake, as your Guatemalan friend will simply step forward to close the gap.
- The sign for "okay" or "all right" (using the thumb and forefinger to make a circle) is seen as an indignity.
- When visiting a Guatemalan home, keep your hands above the table and not on your lap. However, don't put your elbows on the table.
- Pointing with the index finger is considered rude.
- Maintain eye contact, but don't stare.
- The thumbs-up sign is considered an obscene gesture.

*Sensitive Issues*

- Don't criticize your Guatemalan friend in front of others, as this will cause him or her to lose face (become humiliated).

- Don't talk about Guatemalan politics or the violent civil war that ravaged Guatemala for many years.

## MEXICO

*Population:* 101.9 million

*Ethnicity:* Mestizo (60 percent), Amerindian (30 percent), White (9 percent), Other (1 percent)

*Religions/Religious Groups:* Roman Catholic (89 percent), Protestant (6 percent), Other (5 percent)

*Languages:* Spanish, Mayan, and Indigenous

### How to Greet a Mexican

- Use titles with the last name unless you are invited by your Mexican friend to go on a first-name basis. Refer to Mexicans as Señor (Mr.), Señora (Mrs.), or Señorita (Miss), followed by their last name.
- Handshakes are common, although men should wait for a woman to offer her hand first.
- A common phrase for greeting is *"Buenos días"* (pronounced bwey-nohs dee-ahs), which means "Good day."
- See the section on Spain to learn a few phrases in Spanish. This will help create rapport with your Mexican friend.

### Things to Remember When Interacting with a Mexican

- Mexican culture is collectivist. This means that most Mexicans will consider their acceptance of the gospel in light of how it will impact their family and friends. Chances are you may not receive an immediate response, so be patient and supportive of your Mexican friend if he or she struggles spiritually.
- Mexicans often feel Americans have negative attitudes toward them. They also feel that most Americans are cold and insensitive.
- Mexican culture, history, and its natural beauty are all safe topics of conversation.

- Keep in mind that Mexicans are not South Americans. They are part of the North American continent, even though their culture is similar to that of South America.
- A good place to take a Mexican friend for a meal is (obviously) to an authentic Mexican restaurant (not a fast-food restaurant).
- Mexicans have a lot of reverence for churches. If your church allows casual dress, be prepared to explain to your Mexican friend why people are wearing shorts or other informal clothes in church.
- If you are invited to a Mexican home, it is customary to bring flowers. Avoid red or yellow flowers, as red indicates a curse and yellow is associated with mourning.

### Be Aware of These Gestures

- Personal space among Mexicans is smaller than in the United States. When conversing, don't be surprised if your Mexican friend stands closer than you're accustomed to. Backing away is usually a mistake, as your Mexican friend will simply step forward to close the gap.
- The sign for "okay" or "all right" (using the thumb and forefinger to make a circle) is regarded as an indignity.
- Keeping your hands in your pockets while talking is considered rude.
- The thumbs-down sign is an obscene gesture.
- When visiting a Mexican home, keep your hands above the table and not on your lap. However, don't put your elbows on the table.

### Sensitive Issues

- Avoid comparing Mexico to the United States.
- Don't get into immigration issues.
- As with people from most other countries, avoid discussing politics.
- Allow your Mexican friend to save face—never criticize him or her in front of others.
- Avoid talking about the Mexican War (with the United States).

## VENEZUELA

*Population:* 24 million

*Ethnicity:* Mestizo (70 percent), White—including Spanish, Portuguese, and Italian (20 percent), Black (9 percent), and Amerindian (1 percent)

*Religions/Religious Groups:* Roman Catholic (96 percent), Other (4 percent)

*Languages:* Spanish and numerous indigenous dialects

### How to Greet a Venezuelan

- Use titles with the last name unless invited by your Venezuelan friend to go on a first-name basis. Refer to Venezuelans as Señor (Mr.), Señora (Mrs.), or Señorita (Miss), followed by their last name.
- Handshakes are common, although men should wait for a woman to offer her hand first.
- A common phrase for greeting is *"Buenos días"* (pronounced bwey-nohs dee-ahs), which means "Good day."
- An *abrazo,* consisting of a hug, handshake, and several thumps on the shoulder, is usually reserved for close friends.
- See the section on Spain to learn a few phrases in Spanish. This will help create rapport with your Venezuelan friend.

### Things to Remember When Interacting with a Venezuelan

- Venezuelan culture is collectivist. This means that most Venezuelans will consider their acceptance of the gospel in light of how it will impact their family and friends. Chances are you may not receive an immediate response, so be patient and supportive of your Venezuelan friend if he or she struggles spiritually.
- It is safe to talk about Venezuelan culture and history, arts, sports, and food.
- Baseball is a popular sport, and Venezuelans love to talk about it.
- If invited to a Venezuelan home for a meal, follow up by sending a thank-you note, and enclose a nice pen as a gift.
- Venezuelan food typically comprises casseroles and stews. Pasta dishes are also popular.

### *Be Aware of These Gestures*

- Personal space among Venezuelans is smaller than in the United States. When conversing, don't be surprised if your Venezuelan friend stands closer than you're accustomed to. Backing away is usually a mistake, as your Venezuelan friend will simply step forward to close the gap.
- Don't put your feet on top of furniture, books, or other things.
- Maintain eye contact, but don't stare.
- Pointing with the index finger is considered rude.

### *Sensitive Issues*

- As in most other countries, politics is a sensitive issue, so avoid the topic.
- Allow your Venezuelan friend to save face—never criticize him or her in front of others.
- Some Venezuelans may consider you rude if you ask about their family.

# 12

# International Students

In 1954 there were fewer than thirty-five thousand foreign students in the United States. Today there are approximately one-half million foreign students in the United States. They can be found in all fifty states at most of our more than three thousand American colleges and universities.

According to the Institute of International Education, foreign students contribute more than $11 billion to the U.S. economy each year. In 1996 more than one hundred U.S. colleges and universities hosted one thousand or more international students. Consider this: The ten countries that send the largest number of students to the United States are China (11 percent), India (10 percent), Japan (8.5 percent), Korea (8.3 percent), Taiwan (5.2 percent), Canada (4.6 percent), Indonesia (2.1 percent), Thailand (2 percent), Turkey (2 percent), and Mexico (1.9 percent). Now here's the point: Seven of these top-ten countries are either closed to the Christian message or strongly resistant to it.

Think about it. These students are in our neighborhoods, in our schools, in our communities. They are among the brightest and best from their countries. Many who return to their homelands (one estimate says about 80 percent go back) will become political, social, and corporate leaders with tremendous influence. What a ready and waiting field of harvest the Lord has provided for us!

Apart from the United States, the three most populated countries in the world are China, India, and Indonesia. These countries severely restrict missionary activities and are resistant to the gospel. But in the 2000–2001 academic year, these countries enrolled more than 125,000 students in U.S. colleges and universities.

The thirty or so Islamic nations send tens of thousands of students to the United States. To give you one example, Saudi Arabia, which is 100 percent Muslim, enrolled 5,273 students in U.S. colleges and universities during the 2000–2001 academic year. We simply must not ignore this huge and important mission field. We don't have to go to distant lands to bring the gospel to African, Asian, or Middle Eastern people. They are here in our own backyards—in our communities, schools, and workplaces.

*Countries Sending the Greatest Number of Foreign Students to the United States*

| | | | |
|---|---|---|---|
| 1. | China | 6. | Canada |
| 2. | India | 7. | Indonesia |
| 3. | Japan | 8. | Thailand |
| 4. | Korea | 9. | Turkey |
| 5. | Taiwan | 10. | Mexico |

Seven of these countries are either closed to missionaries or are strongly resistant to the gospel.

*Source: Institute of International Education*

If your church doesn't already have a ministry to foreign students, consider starting one. Talk to your church leaders. This becomes more important in areas that are close to cities and large colleges and universities, although people residing anywhere in the United States can effectively reach out to foreign students.

## UNDERSTANDING AND RELATING TO FOREIGN STUDENTS

How do we go about winning foreign students to Jesus? First, review the specific culture- and religion-sensitive guidelines in this book that relate to the person with whom you are building a relationship. Especially keep in mind the following points:

- Rather than a quick witnessing encounter, concentrate on building a *positive relationship* with foreign students. They will be more inclined to hear what you have to say about the gospel if they know you care about them as people. Don't end the relationship if they are unwilling to respond to the gospel. Be patient and gradual in your presentation of the gospel; don't pester them for a decision. Be sensitive to the student and also to the Holy Spirit. You do the sharing, and He will do the convicting.
- Developing a relationship with a foreign student will require time and effort. Be prepared for that.
- Once you find out the student's country of origin and religion, do research to learn as much as you can.
- Bear in mind that when foreign students first come to the United States, they face tremendous emotional pressure—especially culture shock and missing their home, family, and friends.
- Use simple English. Most American slang is lost on foreign students. For many, English is not their first language. Speak slowly and clearly, and use short sentences. Steer clear of the natural tendency to shout when trying to help a student understand what you're saying.
- Keep in mind that these students are among the brightest and best back home and are the future leaders of their countries.

## HOST A FOREIGN STUDENT

Probably the most effective way to reach a foreign student is when he or she first comes to the United States. Many foreign students arrive early—before the semester actually starts—which means colleges must find temporary housing and lodging for them. This is where the church can effectively step in. What if members of a church were to volunteer to host foreign students for a few days or weeks before school starts? This type of need arises just before the fall semester in August and the spring semester in January. You don't even need to be close to the college (if you are willing to drive a couple of hours).

I know of one Mennonite family in Pennsylvania who hosted an Iraqi student for a month before school started. This Iraqi student joined them for devotions and church services and had an opportunity to hear the gospel.

Similarly, foreign students are often at a loss as to what to do during Christmas vacation, Spring break, and Easter break. Imagine the impact if tens of thousands of Christian families were to open their homes during these times to host foreign students!

So how do we start such an outreach? The first step is to see if your church would be interested. Your pastor can present the opportunity, asking volunteer families to list how many students they can host, for how long, and how far they would be willing to drive to pick up and drop off the student. Then the pastor (or designated coordinator) can contact the International Students Office of local colleges and universities and offer to host foreign students, providing a list of host names and phone numbers. It's as simple as that. The International Student Advisor will contact each person on the list individually as needs arise.

If your church is unwilling or unable to take on such a strategy, you can certainly host foreign students on your own. The best time to start contacting schools is in July and early December for students who are arriving for fall and spring semesters, and about three to four weeks before Thanksgiving, spring break, Christmas, and Easter.

## OTHER WAYS TO REACH OUT

- Host an International Students Dinner or International Students Appreciation Day at your church. This works best if your church is within a short driving distance of a school. Make posters and contact the International Student Advisor of the school to see how best to advertise among the foreign students. Have families sign up to provide transportation and host the students for after-church meals.
- Almost all new foreign students attend a college orientation, but they also need help to open a bank account, shop at a "superstore" for groceries for the first time, and so on. See if you and others from your church can volunteer for these activities.

- One Christian from Michigan hosted a monthly "dialogue" time in his home. He invited international students from nearby colleges and universities and either proposed a stimulating topic for discussion or simply allowed the evening to unfold spontaneously. On average, about twenty students participated. He always provided a light supper. (Free meals were popular—an opportunity to escape cafeteria food!) Hosting these monthly dialogues gave him incredible insight into many cultures through the eyes of the students who attended.

- Invite a foreign student to your home and prepare a dish from his or her home country. Better yet, perhaps the two of you could prepare a meal together—a great relationship builder!

- Find out if there are any cultural or ethnic associations in your city or county. See if you can get involved in an area that reaches out to foreign students.

- If you have time, volunteer with the International Students Office at your local college or university. If there are others among your friends, family, or church community who can also volunteer time, do this as a group. Help is especially needed during the beginning of each semester. You can also volunteer for other events that the International Students Office may organize throughout the year. This will help you connect with the students.

- If you or your church can organize a free English class, advertise it among foreign students and also to other ethnic or cultural associations in your community.

- One church near Philadelphia holds a monthly International Students Brunch after their Sunday service. Dozens show up each time, many of them first-timers.

- Many foreign students live with other foreign students and share the rent. They are often in need of household items, electronic appliances, furniture, and so on. One church asks its members to donate any items in good condition to the International Student Office. They make a list with the phone number of the person donating the item, and the college circulates the list to the foreign students.

- If there are places of historic interest where you live, organize a tour for foreign students. Consult with the International Students Office before you do this. The school might even be willing to provide a van and a driver.
- Once a student has returned home, you can continue your relationship through letters and e-mail. However, be careful what you write, especially about religion, to closed countries such as China and Indonesia. If in doubt, ask the student.

Most of us have abundant opportunities to develop friendships with international students if only we'll take the initiative. It is amazing to think that all of us can be "missionaries" with great influence on foreign countries without ever leaving our communities. Pray that God would use you to reach many students who very well might be future leaders in their homelands.

Part 3

# How to Present
# the Gospel to People
# of Other Religions

# 13

# General Guidelines for Interacting with People of Other Religions

This section provides help for relating to people of other religions and for eventually telling them about Jesus Christ. Specific guidelines for the major countries of the world are provided in the preceding chapters, while specific guidelines for the major world religions are provided in the chapters that follow. The guidelines presented are *general* and apply in *most* circumstances. In your interactions, you may find that some people are exceptions.

As we begin this section, keep in mind the following universal guidelines:

1. *Show respect for places of worship.* Hindus, Muslims, and Buddhists usually do not wear shoes into their places of worship. They also dress modestly, and there is a general air of reverence in temples and mosques. It is very hard for these people to understand why contemporary churches are so "irreverent," and it can be shocking for them to see worshipers wearing hats, jeans, or shorts inside church. Applause and whistling, as well as clapping during music, can also be jarring. Be prepared to explain why these practices are acceptable in your church.

2. *Show respect for scriptures.* In most countries, people have a lot of reverence for their scriptures—not just the content, but the actual book

itself. For instance, if a Hindu were to drop a copy of the *Bhagavad-Gita* by mistake or let it touch his or her feet, he or she would be horrified. The offender would say a sincere prayer asking for forgiveness and then kiss the book. When you're with international friends, treat the Bible as well as the sacred texts of other religions with respect.

3. *Never ridicule or belittle.* Perhaps it goes without saying, but the point is so important that I'll mention it anyway: Do not belittle other people's religions, gods, or religious idols and symbols (even under the guise of "just kidding" or "poking fun"). Never. Period.

4. *Avoid arguments.* Your job is to proclaim the gospel, not to win an argument. If you feel a conversation is becoming argumentative, drop the subject and pick it up later.

5. *Show respect for customs and traditions.* When visiting people's homes, do not touch or lean on idols or pictures of gods and goddesses. This is considered extremely rude.

6. *Build a relationship.* Reaching someone from another culture and/or religion often requires time, but it is well worth the effort. Concentrate on building a friendship. Keep in mind that there could be serious consequences for the person who forsakes his or her faith, including being disowned by family and community. Be patient and supportive, as any good friend would be.

7. *Share your testimony.* When sharing your personal testimony, keep it short and to the point. Avoid Christian terms that non-Christians would find meaningless, such as *convicted, born again, filled with the Holy Spirit,* and so on. Start your testimony with an attention-grabbing statement, and explain why following Christ made sense to you and how serving Him has made a difference in your life. Use the gulf diagram (discussed later in this section) for a simple representation of the gospel.

Always keep a smile on your face, soak your attempts with prayer, and don't forget Who does the saving. Review the briefing material for your friend's religion before you start any dialogue.

# 14

# Hindus

- There are more than 800 million Hindus in the world today, mostly in India and Nepal.
- Hinduism is the world's third largest religion after Christianity and Islam.
- When a Hindu dies, the body is cremated and the ashes are cast into a sacred river.
- About 1.3 million Hindus live in the United States. Another 100,000 live in Canada.
- Hinduism readily absorbs teachings from other religions and has been described by some as a "user-friendly" religion.
- Most Hindus live in the following countries: Bangladesh, Bhutan, the Fiji Islands, India, Mauritius, Nepal, South Africa, Sri Lanka, Trinidad, and the United Kingdom.

ORIGIN

Hinduism, one of the oldest religions in the world, can be traced back thousands of years. It has no one single founder. Over the centuries the many teachings and interpretations of countless gurus and teachers have evolved into what Hinduism is today. The *Vedic* texts were the source and cause for the practice of the Vedic religion. Hinduism evolved as a result of the practice of this religion.

## Sacred Texts

The sacred texts of Hinduism can be divided into two main parts, much like our Old and New Testaments. However, unlike Christianity where the New Testament is an extension and fulfillment of the Old Testament, the two parts of Hinduism combine to form one text, though with many parts.

### The Age of the Vedas

The time period of these texts started anywhere between 2500 and 1500 B.C. and ended around 600 B.C., although the exact dates are a hotly debated issue among Hindu scholars. The literature of this time period is known as the *Vedas* (which can also be translated to mean "knowledge"). The Vedas are divided into four parts:

1. *The Rig Veda.* The oldest and most important Veda. It means "praise" in Sanskrit. It is a collection of 1,028 hymns divided into ten books. It is considered by many Hindus to be the holiest of all Hindu texts.

2. *The Soma Veda.* This Veda contains 1,529 verses and is mainly derived from the *Rig Veda,* although the verses have been set to rhythm. Some scholars consider this text to be the beginning of classical Indian music.

3. *The Yajur Veda.* This Veda describes the art of sacrifice. It explains the oneness of God with creation and that gods can be celebrated with periodic offerings. It describes how to make sacrifices and offerings.

4. *The Atharva Veda.* This Veda, written by the priest Atharvan, is made up of 730 hymns, including charms, poetry, and curses. These hymns are meant to guide a person in daily living.

Most of the beliefs and customs of modern-day Hinduism have evolved out of the Vedas, although they have been modified from time to time. There is considerable freedom for the individual to choose what he or she may want to practice.

## The Age of the Epics

The Epic Age began after the Age of the Vedas and ended around A.D. 200. There are three epics in Hinduism:

1. *Mahabharata* (including the *Bhagavad-Gita*). This is the story of the five Pandava brothers and their many struggles and victories. In a certain battle one of the brothers faces the difficult task of fighting against his kinsmen. At this point his charioteer, Krishna (who is an incarnation of the god Vishnu), engages in a 700-verse dialogue with him. It is one of the most popular portions of Hindu texts. The entire *Mahabharata* is made up of 106,000 verses.

2. *Ramayana*. This is the story of King Rama (another incarnation of the god Vishnu), his wife, Sita, and brother Laksman.

3. The *Puranas*. This literally means "ancient narratives." It is intended for the average Hindu and deals primarily with *bhakti* (devotion to a god) and *dharma* (doing one's personal and social duty).

## BELIEFS AND PRACTICES

Sarvepalli Radhakrishnan, former president of India and a great Hindu scholar, wrote in his acclaimed work *The Hindu View of Life*, "There has been no such thing as a uniform, stationary, unalterable Hinduism whether in point of belief or practice. Hinduism is a movement, not a position; a process, not a result; a growing tradition, not a fixed revelation."

### What Do Those Titles Mean?

*Acharya:* A religious scholar

*Guru:* A spiritual leader

*Sadhu:* A holy man

*Purohit* (Priest): Can mean different things, usually someone who is trained to perform rituals.

Contrary to what many assume, Hindus believe in one supreme God, their Supreme Being, who is one with the universe (also known as the *Brahmana*). However, their many gods and goddesses represent the different forms or aspects of that one God.

Hindus believe the divinity of the one God passes through all creation. Imagine it as a necklace with many pearls on it. The thread that passes through the pearls is their one God. The many pearls are the different forms of creation.

Hindus do not believe that the creation of the universe took place at one point. There is no beginning or end. The universe is in a constant process of creation and disintegration.

Hindus also believe that we are all caught in the cycle of birth and rebirth, which is determined by good or bad deeds in the past. In other words, if you perform a lot of good deeds in this life, you may be born again as a human being

---

*Popular Hindu Gods and Goddesses*

The following three gods are referred to as the "Holy Trinity":

*Brahma*—the god of creation

*Vishnu*—the god responsible for the protection and preservation of the universe. Hindus believe that Vishnu has appeared on earth in many forms, two of the most famous being Rama and Krishna.

*Shiva*—the god responsible for destruction and regeneration

Other important gods and goddesses include:

*Krishna*—an incarnation of Vishnu

*Lakhsmi*—the goddess of wealth and prosperity

*Saraswati*—the goddess of wisdom

*Agni*—the god of fire

*Pavan*—the god of wind

*Ganesh*—the god with the head of an elephant, who is responsible for removing obstacles

or achieve salvation by being released from the cycle of birth and rebirth to become one with the universe. If you do a lot of bad deeds, you end up being reborn as a lower life-form (an animal or, worse, an insect).

Hindus have a difficult time defining salvation because being released from the cycle of birth and rebirth and becoming one with the universe is considered to be a state of inexpressible bliss. Of course, this means that there is no heaven or hell. Some Hindus believe there are several "layers" of heavens and hells where souls reside briefly in between the cycles of birth and rebirth. However, many Hindus will describe hell as being in the cycle of birth and rebirth or sometimes the suffering that afflicts bad people between births.

Hinduism also has an elaborate caste system. At certain times in Indian history, the caste system became oppressive; the higher castes enjoyed privileges that were denied to the lower castes and the "untouchables." Many scholars believe this system helped in the birth and spreading of reform religions such as Buddhism and Jainism. However, it is important to note that today castes come into play mostly with regard to marriages, although a significant number of lower-caste people and untouchables are still bypassed by society.

### Articles of Faith
A Hindu embraces some or all of these tenets of faith:
- belief in one Supreme Being who is one with the universe but has manifested himself in numerous gods and goddesses
- belief that there are many ways to God and that no one particular religion teaches the only way to God
- belief in idol worship
- belief in reincarnation (the cycle of birth and rebirth)
- belief in *ahimsa,* or nonviolence, as the highest virtue
- belief in *karma*—the law of cause and effect (our actions, speech, and thoughts create our destiny)
- belief in working toward achieving salvation from the cycle of birth and rebirth
- belief in the divinity of the Vedas and that one should study them regularly

- belief that the universe is eternal, without beginning or end
- belief that one should offer regular *puja* or worship to the deities

## THE SPECIFICS

1. *God.* There is one God (the Supreme Being) who has appeared and continues to appear in many forms. Hence, the numerous gods and goddesses. The Hindu Supreme Being is impersonal and unknowable. (Some Hindus may argue that you can know the one God through the many gods and goddesses.)

2. *Creation.* There is no creation story in Hinduism. The universe has been in continuous existence and is in a constant state of creation and disintegration.

3. *Sin.* Since there is no creation story or fall of humankind, there is no concept of original sin. Each person does bad deeds or good deeds and will pay for it accordingly by being punished with a lower life-form or by being rewarded with a higher life-form or salvation.

4. *Salvation.* Salvation is the liberation of the soul from the cycle of birth and rebirth and becoming one with the Supreme Being or with the universe in a continuous state of inexpressible bliss.

## HOW TO WITNESS TO A HINDU

In recent years Hinduism has found great appeal in Western society. At present there are more than one million Hindus in the United States. Keep in mind that

### ISKCON

Srila Prabhupada founded the International Society for Krishna Consciousness in 1966 in New York. It quickly gained in popularity. ISKCON members worship Krishna, an incarnation of Vishnu. They can be easily spotted by their saffron-colored clothes. (Hindus consider saffron a sacred color.) Male ISKCON members shave their heads, leaving a ponytail. The base of the ponytail is considered a sacred spot. ISKCON has hundreds of temples in more than seventy countries.

when a Hindu hears the gospel, more often than not he or she will gladly accept Christ as *a* god, but not as *the* God. To many Hindus, Christianity is regarded as a very "narrow-minded" religion that maintains the exclusivity of Christ as the only God through whom humankind can be saved.

Before you continue, make sure you have read chapter 13 for general guidelines. Also, review the country-specific information presented in part 2 so that you are aware of additional culture-specific customs and worldviews. Remember that this is not an exhaustive treatment of the subject, but a quick snapshot.

### The God/Man Separation Issue

One of the core aspirations of a Hindu is to find the *inner self* in an effort to escape the cycle of death and rebirth into another life-form. When one finds the inner self, one is able to resolve the age-old mystery of the cycle of life, death, and rebirth. Ironically, when someone does find his or her inner self, he or she is confronted with the sinful nature and the realization of helplessness and the need for a savior.

One of the best and simplest ways to communicate the gospel is through the gulf diagram* that shows the gulf of sin separating God and man. In Christianity, we believe that by His death on the cross, Jesus Christ bridged the gulf of sin that separates us from God, making it possible for us to know God and have a relationship with Him.

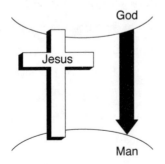

With this simple diagram in mind, let's see what Hinduism says:

---

\* Special thanks to *NewLife* Publications for permission to use the gulf diagram from *Have You Heard of the Four Spiritual Laws?* © Copyright 1965, 1994, 2000 by Bill Bright, *NewLife* Publications, Campus Crusade for Christ. All rights reserved. Used by permission.

|  | God | Chasm | Bridge | Salvation |
|---|---|---|---|---|
| **Christianity** | Personal, knowable | Sin | Christ | Eternity with God in heaven |
| **Hinduism** | Impersonal | Wrong deeds of past life | Good deeds in this life | Becoming one with the universe (no heaven) |

Once you study this chart, you will be able to provide a credible case as to why following Christ makes sense. For example, how can one have a relationship with an impersonal God? Can anyone be perfect or good enough to bridge the gap? Even if, through some extraordinary herculean effort, a person managed to achieve a short span of time doing nothing but good deeds, can anyone sustain this without ever stumbling for the rest of his or her life? What does "becoming one with the universe" really mean?

Broach the topic of the cycle of birth and rebirth and salvation. Listen first. Then offer the explanation that Christ provides an answer to how salvation can be achieved. It is difficult for a Hindu to accept that salvation can be attained without any work on the individual's part. Ask, "Can anyone be perfect or good enough to achieve salvation by his or her own means?"

Some other questions to pose:

1. *God.* How is it possible to worship a god whom you cannot know?
2. *Creation.* How did we get here? How did the universe get its present form? If the universe had no beginning (as Hindus believe), how is it that scientists have proven that the universe is slowing down? How did the different forms of life on earth get here?
3. *Sin.* How do you explain man's sinful nature? (Having no original sin concept and believing that each human being has an inherent divinity inside of him or her, this one is especially tough for many Hindus to explain.) If we are all divine and if we don't believe in original sin, then why is there evil in this world? Why is there sin? Why do men and women do things that are clearly wrong? Why are men and women different from the rest of creation?

*Keep in Mind...*

Here are some specific guidelines to keep in mind when sharing the gospel with
Hindus:

- Follow the 1 Peter 3:15 model as described in chapter 2 of this book.
- Never take your Hindu friend to a hamburger place to talk. The Hindu
  religion considers the cow to be a holy animal, so eating beef is out of
  the question. A Hindu would be greatly insulted to be invited to a
  restaurant where beef is served. By the same token, most Hindus avoid
  leather products. Many Hindus are vegetarians.
- Stay away from the temptation to label Hindu gods and goddesses as
  evil spirits or demons. Think of it this way: If a Hindu were to tell
  you that Jesus is an evil god and that Hinduism is the only way to
  salvation, how open would you be to hearing anything about Hinduism after that point? Many well-meaning but zealous Christians
  have turned off their Hindu friends by making this one simple, devastating error.
- Respect, respect, respect! Never make fun of or otherwise denigrate the
  Hindu belief in many gods and goddesses or in their unusual anatomy.
  Doing so would be a sure way to turn off your listener.
- Christians who were once Hindus will often say that the most convincing argument for following Christ was the patient, consistent love
  Christians showed them.
- The word *trinity* is not unknown to a Hindu. However, its meaning is
  very different. The Hindus consider the holy trinity to be the three
  important gods—Brahma, Vishnu, and Shiva. In most circumstances,
  you will probably not need to use this word until later, but keep in
  mind the difference in meaning.
- Keep a smile on your face, and change the subject as soon as you see
  the discussion turning into an argument. We rarely win someone to
  Christ by arguing or debating with them. Change the topic, reaffirm
  your love and friendship, and postpone the spiritual discussion for
  another time.

- Share your personal testimony. This can be a powerful tool in the hands of the Holy Spirit. Prepare your testimony in advance, and keep it short and simple. Don't use words or phrases such as *convicted, filled with the Spirit,* and *born again,* which are meaningless to a Hindu.
- Don't forget Who does the saving.

## ORGANIZATIONS

Himalayan Academy
107 Kaholalele Road
Kapaa, HI 96746
www.himalayanacademy.com

*Hinduism Today* magazine
107 Kaholalele Road
Kapaa, HI 96746-9304
www.hinduismtoday.org

International Society for Krishna Consciousness (ISKCON)
P.O. Box 1119
Alachua, FL 32615
www.iskcon.org

Ramakrishna-Vivekananda Center
17 East 94th Street
New York, NY 10128
www.ramakrishna.org

## FURTHER READING

Eastman, Roger, ed. *The Ways of Religion.* 3d ed. New York: Oxford University Press, 1999.

Embree, Ainslie, and Stephen N. Hay, eds. *Sources of Indian Tradition.* 2d ed. 2 vols. New York: Columbia University Press, 1988.

Goswami, Mukunda, and Malory Nye. *Inside the Hare Krishna Movement.* Badger, Calif.: Torchlight Publishing, 2001.

Hamilton, Sue. *Indian Philosophy: A Very Short Introduction.* Oxford, U.K.: Oxford University Press, 2001.

Kanitakara, Hermanta, W. Owen Cole, and V. P. Kanitar. *Teach Yourself Hinduism.* New York: McGraw-Hill, Contemporary Books, 1996.

Kingsland, Venika M. *The Simple Guide to Hinduism.* Folkestone, Kent, U.K.: Global Books, 1997.

Knipe, David M. *Hinduism: Experiments in the Sacred.* San Francisco: Harper-SanFrancisco, 1991.

Knott, Kim. *Hinduism: A Very Short Introduction.* New York: Oxford University Press, 2000.

McDowell, Josh. *Evidence That Demands a Verdict.* 2 vols. Nashville: Nelson, 1993.

O'Flaherty, Wendy. *Hindu Myths.* Baltimore: Penguin, 1975.

Strobel, Lee. *The Case for Christ.* Grand Rapids: Zondervan, 1998.

# 15

# Muslims

- *Islam* is the name of the religion; a *Muslim* is a person who follows Islam.
- More than one billion people in the world are Muslims.
- Islam is the fastest growing religion in the United States and throughout the world.
- The Muslim holy book is called the *Qur'an*.
- Muslims hope their good works outweigh their bad works. As such, they do not have an absolute assurance of salvation.
- Muslims believe Jesus was a prophet.
- Muslims follow a lunar calendar containing twelve months with eleven fewer days than the Western calendar. Each of the twelve months has religious significance. Perhaps the best known among them is the month of Ramadan, the month of fasting.
- During Ramadan, Muslims do not eat between sunrise and sunset.
- Although Muslims regard Muhammad as a prophet and the founder of Islam, they do not regard him as a god.
- Mainstream Islam in North America and many other countries is quite different from the beliefs and practices of Muslim extremists. It is not violent or brutal.

- Between five and seven million Muslims live in the United States.
- Most Muslims live in Africa, central and southern Asia, and the Middle East.

*The Number of Muslims in America*
**1970**—0.5 million
**2001**—6–7 million

*Source:* Time, *1 October 2001.*

## ORIGIN

Muhammad was born in 570 C.E. His father died before he was born, and his mother died when he was still a young child. He was raised by his grandfather. Even as a young man, Muhammad got involved in the flourishing caravan trade of Mecca (in Saudi Arabia). Mecca was the commercial center of trading between the Indian subcontinent and the countries around the Mediterranean. However, in the midst of an economic boom, Mecca was experiencing some intense social, moral, and spiritual upheavals.

Muhammad became the business manager (to borrow a modern term) of a wealthy widow, Khadija. Islamic tradition maintains that Muhammad was twenty-five and Khadija was forty when they got married. They had several sons and daughters, but none of the sons survived.

During this time Muhammad would often retreat to a cave outside of town to meditate. When he was approximately forty years of age, during the month of Ramadan, Muhammad transitioned from "Muhammad the trader" to "Muhammad the prophet," receiving a revelation from Allah through the angel Gabriel. Over the next twenty-two years, he received many more revelations. The collected messages received by Muhammad are contained in the *Qur'an,* the holy scriptures of Islam.

Although initially he had a hard time preaching to his fellow Meccans, within a short time Muhammad was able to transform a small band of faithful followers into a powerful religious community. He was also a successful military leader and defeated the Persian and Iraqi armies. By the time he died in 632 C.E., Islam had spread across Arabia.

*Countries with the Largest Muslim Population*

| | | |
|---|---|---|
| 1. | Indonesia | 181 million |
| 2. | Pakistan | 141 million |
| 3. | India | 124 million |
| 4. | Bangladesh | 111 million |
| 5. | Turkey | 66 million |
| 6. | Egypt | 66 million |
| 7. | Iran | 65 million |
| 8. | Nigeria | 63 million |
| 9. | China | 38 million |
| 10. | Algeria | 31 million |

About 40 percent of Muslims live in South and Southeast Asia; 30 percent live in Africa.

*Source:* National Geographic, *January 2002.*

## SACRED TEXTS

There are two parts to the sacred texts of Islam.

### 1. The Qur'an

The *Qur'an* is the verbatim collection of revelations Allah gave to Muhammad. Muhammad compiled most of the chapters; the rest were completed after his death. The *Qur'an* comprises 114 chapters, or *suras,* and is shorter than the New Testament. The early chapters are the shortest and portray Muhammad's struggles in his quest for spiritual truth and meaning. The chapters get longer toward the end and are filled with instructions on living the Muslim life.

Muslims are very respectful of the *Qur'an's* teachings and of the physical book itself. The book is not to be treated irreverently and cannot be touched by someone who is ritually unclean (such as women who are menstruating). The words *Islam* and *Muslim* are found in the *Qur'an*. Islam means "surrender" of one's will to Allah's will. Many Muslims find it offensive to be referred to as *Mohammadans* because they do not worship Muhammad.

Muslims believe that the Scriptures of the Jews and the Christians talk about the same God the *Qur'an* talks about. However, they also believe that the Bible has been corrupted. They believe that the *Qur'an* represents the most complete and accurate teachings of Allah.

## 2. Hadith

Many stories and teachings of Muhammad began circulating after his death. Muslims believe that Muhammad was faultless and that he had numerous virtues. These stories and teachings were collected into a book called the *Hadith*. It is quite similar to the parables in the Bible. However, it is important to keep in mind that although the *Hadith* is regarded as an excellent guidebook for life, it is not considered to have the same kind of divine inspiration as the *Qur'an*.

## BELIEFS AND PRACTICES

As mentioned above, Islam literally means "surrender" or "submission" to the will of Allah; thus a Muslim is one who surrenders his will to the will of Allah. In fact, in order to be a Muslim one need only affirm, "There is no God but the one God [Allah], and Muhammad is his prophet."

## Articles of Faith

Basic tenets of Islam include:

- *Belief in one God.* Muslims are strictly monotheistic. There is only one God: Allah. Allah is omnipotent and omniscient. Some Muslims consider Christians to be polytheistic because we seem to believe in more than one God (Father, Son, and Holy Spirit).
- *Belief in angels and demons.* Muslims believe that there are angels and demons (fallen angels).
- *Belief in prophets.* Muslims believe Abraham, Moses, Jesus, and Muhammad were a few of the many prophets Allah sent to the world. Jesus was

a prophet, but not the Savior. Muhammad was the last and the greatest of all prophets, and the *Qur'an* supercedes all other revelations.

- *Belief in a Day of Judgment.* Muslims believe there will be a Day of Judgment on which each person's deeds will be weighed. True believers will go to heaven, a place of spiritual as well as physical pleasures. Non-believers will burn in the fire of hell.
- *Belief in the will of Allah.* Muslims believe everything happens according to the will and permission of Allah. Muslims believe they can know the will of Allah by following Islamic principles closely.

### The Five Pillars of Islam

Muslims express their worship by following the five pillars of Islam:

1. *Shahadah* (Confession of Faith). If a person, out of his or her own conviction, says the following words, then he or she becomes a Muslim: "There is no God but the one God [Allah], and Muhammad is His prophet." This must be stated from a person's own free will at least once in his lifetime.

2. *Salat* (Worship). Every adult Muslim must pray five times daily facing the holy city of Mecca. Mosques often have a niche carved out on the wall facing Mecca so people can face the right way while worshiping. The five prayers should be offered at sunrise, noon, afternoon, sunset, and night.

3. *Zakat* (Sharing Wealth). Muslims are obligated to share 2.5 percent of their income and some possessions with the poor and needy.

4. *Siyam* (Fasting). Fasting occurs during the entire month of Ramadan. Muslims are to abstain from food and drink all day from dawn to dusk.

5. *Hajj* (Pilgrimage). All Muslims who can undertake the journey physically and financially are obligated to make a pilgrimage to the holy city of Mecca, in Saudi Arabia, at least once in their lifetime. About 2.5 million Muslims make the trip each year. The Saudi government provides housing and food for the pilgrims.

It is important to note some additional teachings of Islam. Muslims do not consume alcohol or pork. Gambling is not allowed. Muslims are also prohibited from eating animals that have either died on their own, were killed by other animals, or were improperly slaughtered.

They believe life on earth is a period of testing for the life to come. No person or nation is chosen by God; all humans are equal in the sight of Allah. Jews and Christians received earlier revelations from Allah through messengers such as Abraham, Moses, Jesus, and others. Hence, Jews and Christians are also referred to as *Ahl-al-Kitab,* or "People of the Book" or revealed Scriptures. However, these earlier revelations are not considered to be as pure or as correct as the *Qur'an.*

Allah, then, is the same God Jews and Christians worship: Jehovah. However, Allah did not come to earth in human form; therefore Jesus cannot be His son. In fact, to believe that God had a son is sacrilegious. To Muslims, Jesus was just a prophet. God cannot have a son. For this reason it is never appropriate to refer to Allah as "Father."

It is also important to note that most American Muslims follow mainstream Islamic teachings. They are peace-loving, devout, hard-working people. This is quite different from the principles espoused by Muslim extremists.

### The Divisions

There are two major sects within Islam: Sunni Muslims and Shi'ite Muslims. (There is a smaller but significant third group, the Sufis, and other very small sects.)

1. *Sunni Muslims.* Most Muslims (about 90 percent) are Sunni Muslims. They tend to be "predestinarians," believing that nothing happens on earth outside of the will and permission of Allah. They have been able to adapt to various cultures, although they strongly emphasize the importance of Islamic law. They differ with the Shi'ites in leadership disputes, but from a doctrinal viewpoint there is not much difference between the two.

2. *Shi'ite Muslims.* Shi'ites believe in *Imams* or "perfect teachers" who came after Muhammad. They promote a strict interpretation of the

*Qur'an.* Shi'ites split from the Sunnis over a dispute about Muhammad's successors. They tend to believe more in man's free will and the value of human reason. They live mostly in Iran. Most Iranian Americans are Shi'ites.

3. *Sufism.* This small, mystical division of Islam emphasizes a personal relationship with Allah. They practice meditation and ritual dancing as a way to know Allah. Rumi, whose works are popular in the West, was a Sufi.

## The Specifics

1. *God.* There is one God, and His name is Allah. He is omniscient and omnipotent and is the Creator of the universe. He is the same as the Jewish and Christian God: Jehovah.

2. *Prophets.* Allah has made His will known through numerous messengers or prophets. These include Abraham, Moses, Jesus, and Muhammad.

3. *Sin.* There is no concept of original sin. God will not punish all humankind for the sins committed by Adam and Eve. Each person is responsible for his or her own life, and Allah does not need to reincarnate and sacrifice Himself for the sins of His creation.

4. *Salvation.* Muslims believe that there are two angels keeping a record of everyone's good and bad deeds. Muslims are never certain which way the scales will tilt; they can only hope that one day the good deeds will outweigh the bad deeds. Allah will decide on the Day of Judgment who has lived according to His will and who has not.

## How to Witness to a Muslim

It is imperative that Christians take the gospel with love and respect to every Muslim in America. As mentioned earlier, Islam is the fastest growing religion in the world *and in the United States.* There are more Muslims in America than there are Seventh-Day Adventists, Mennonites, Jehovah's Witnesses, Unitarians, Assemblies of God members, and Evangelical Free Church members *combined.*

Islam is on the verge of overtaking Judaism as the largest non-Christian religion in America. Muslims outnumber Presbyterians, Mormons, and Episcopalians. In the 1960s there were hardly any mosques in the United States. That number has grown to more than two thousand today, according to the Council on American-Islamic Relations. The U.S. Department of State estimates the number of converts in U.S. mosques to be approximately 30 percent. The number of mosques has grown 25 percent between 1994 and 2000.

At the time of this writing, there are many more mosques being built across the country. A $15 million, sixty-five-thousand-square-foot Islamic Center of America, one of the largest mosques in America, is scheduled to open in Michigan in 2004. The entire budget is being financed through private donations. A McDonald's restaurant in Michigan now offers *halal* McNuggets (lawful meat that is prepared according to the Islamic law).

It has never been more important for us to understand Islam and how we can effectively share the good news of Jesus Christ with its followers. Arguably, Muslims are among the toughest people to witness to. But we serve a powerful and living God who is on our side. With His help and the Holy Spirit's convicting power, we can see the impossible happen!

Before you continue, make sure you have read chapter 13 for general guidelines. Also, review the country-specific information presented in part 2 so that you are aware of additional culture-specific customs and worldviews. Keep in mind that this is not an exhaustive treatment of the subject, but a quick snapshot view.

### Begin with Points of Agreement

Always try to begin a conversation about your faith by underscoring the points on which Islam and Christianity agree. For instance:

- *Jesus was sinless.* Muslims believe Jesus lived without sin. In fact, the *Qur'an* contains at least thirty-five direct references to Jesus. Apart from Muhammad, Jesus is considered to be the most important prophet. This is a good point to start with. Can any man live a life without sin? Obviously, there was something different about Jesus. Find out what your Muslim friend thinks about Jesus. Bring out the verses from the Gospels that underscore what Christ said about Himself.

Your Muslim friend may say the *Qur'an* is more accurate than the New Testament, so start by reading about the miracles of Jesus in the *Qur'an*. (Look at the index of any English *Qur'an* for a listing of the miracles performed by Jesus, such as healing the sick, restoring the sight of the blind, and raising people from the dead.) Reflect on how no other prophet performed the kind of miracles Jesus did.

- *One God.* Islam is a strictly monotheistic religion.
- *Eternal God.* God is omnipotent and omniscient and the Creator of the universe.
- *Creation.* God created the universe out of nothing.
- *Prophets.* Muslims believe in Abraham and Moses.
- *The Virgin Birth.* The *Qur'an* mentions that God sent an angel to Mary and told her she would be the mother of a prophet. Mary was a virgin when she conceived Jesus. However, Muslims do not believe that this makes Jesus the Son of God.
- *The holiness of Jesus.* Islam teaches that Jesus was worthy of regard in this world and hereafter. Many Muslims revere Jesus.
- *Equality of all humankind.* Islam teaches all are equal before God, regardless of race and nationality.

### Prepare for Points of Disagreement

Be aware of the points of disagreement between Islam and Christianity. I've posed several Christian beliefs below, followed by the typical Muslim reaction. There are a number of good books that suggest helpful responses to these Muslim reactions, and I strongly suggest you use them in your preparation. Two that I highly recommend are Lee Strobel's *The Case for Christ* and Josh McDowell's *Evidence That Demands a Verdict*.

- *Original sin.* Muslim reaction: "How can a good God punish the entire human race for the sins of two people? Sure, Adam and Eve sinned and every person on earth sins, but we don't inherit a sinful nature; each person is responsible for his or her own life. And since we aren't born with a sinful nature, then obviously no savior is needed. Jesus came as a prophet, not as a savior."

- *Jesus is God.* Muslim reaction: "Jesus was a holy man, but he was not God. Jesus is worthy of respect, but not of worship. God is infinite; Jesus was not. Jesus cannot be eternal because he was born only two thousand years ago. He himself worshiped God, so how can he be God?"
- *Jesus is the Son of God.* Muslim reaction: "God cannot have a child; God is indivisible. Spiritual as well as physical parenthood of God is inconceivable."
- *Jesus died on the cross and rose from the dead.* Muslim reaction: "Jesus did not die on the cross and did not rise from the dead. Maybe it was someone else. The disciples may have been mistaken. Even if it was Jesus, he certainly did not rise from the dead. He may have fainted, or the disciples may have stolen his body. Since Jesus was not able to save himself from persecution, how can he be God?"
- *Fulfillment of the promise God made to Abraham.* Muslim reaction: "Ishmael, not Isaac, fulfilled the promises God made to Abraham."

### The God/Man Separation Issue

One of the best and simplest ways to communicate the gospel is through the gulf diagram that shows the gulf of sin separating God and man. In Christianity, we believe that, by His death on the cross, Jesus Christ bridged the gulf of sin that separates us from God, making it possible for us to know God and have a relationship with Him. (See the gulf diagram on page 189.)

With that simple diagram in mind, let's consider what Islam says:

|  | God | Chasm | Bridge | Salvation |
|---|---|---|---|---|
| Christianity | Personal, knowable | Sin | Christ | Eternity with God in heaven |
| Islam | Sunnis and Shi'ites— Impersonal Sufis— Personal | Sin | More good deeds than bad deeds | Paradise (a place of both physical and spiritual pleasure) |

Muslims do not believe that man is born with a sin nature. According to Islam, Satan drives people to sin, but ultimately we are all responsible for our own lives. On the Day of Judgment, Allah will weigh each person's good and bad deeds. If the scales tip toward the good deeds, you will enter paradise; if not, you will enter hell. As you can see, barring a few exceptions, most Muslims are never sure of their salvation. They can only hope that at the end of life their good deeds will outweigh their bad deeds.

Once you study this chapter and the chart, you will be able to provide a credible case as to why following Christ makes sense. For example, how can one have a relationship with an impersonal God? Can anyone be perfect or good enough to bridge the gap? Even if, through some extraordinary herculean effort, a person manages to achieve a short span of time doing nothing but good deeds, can anyone sustain this without ever stumbling for the rest of his or her life? How can one ever be sure of salvation? (Of course, the answer from an Islamic point of view is that one can never be sure.)

Do some good deeds carry more weight than others? What about bad deeds—are some sins greater than others? In the scales of life, do murder and lying carry the same weight? (If so, then no one can even begin to guess to which side the scales will tip.) Doesn't it make sense that a perfect God would view every sin as sin, no matter how small we may think it is? And can we ever become perfect enough to cover all of our imperfections?

It is important to note a common misconception we have about Muslims. Due in large part to the media's focus on Islamic extremists, it is easy to stereotype the Islamic faith as a religion of terrorists and assume that all Muslims hold extreme views. Yet the vast majority of Muslims in America do not share these views or have any connection with these groups. On the contrary, most American Muslims are peaceloving and tolerant toward people of other faiths, and they hold strongly traditional family and moral values.

Another misconception we have is that most, if not all, Muslims in America are of Middle Eastern origin. Less than 15 percent of Muslims in America are Middle Easterners. African Americans (42 percent) and South Asians (24 percent) make up the two largest groups among American Muslims. There are also a growing number of whites converting to Islam. More than eighty thousand Muslims in America are of Western European descent. In a survey of more than twelve hundred mosques conducted by the Council on American-Islamic Relations in the year 2000, it was revealed that 27 percent of converts attending these mosques were whites.

We must be careful to evaluate our own stereotypes before we can effectively witness to Muslims. There are a lot of true seekers among Muslims in America. Let's shed our stereotypes, drop our biases, and see Muslims for who they truly are: people created by God, who are loved by Him, and who need to know Christ.

Some questions to pose:

1. *God* (for Sunni and Shi'ite Muslims). How is it possible to worship a god whom you cannot know and have a personal relationship with?

2. *Sin.* How do you explain man's sinful nature? If we don't have a sinful nature and if we don't believe in original sin, then why is there evil in this world? Why do men and women do things that are clearly wrong? If Satan has the power to drive us to sin, shouldn't God have greater power to save us from the ultimate consequence of sin— eternal death? But if we are simply to hope our good works will save us, then what has God done to save us?

Since salvation is dependent upon each person, what has Allah done to save us? Sure, He provided guidelines, but from a Christian viewpoint, God provided a way that cost Him something priceless.

*Keep in Mind...*

Here are some additional specific guidelines to keep in mind when sharing with Muslims:

• Follow the 1 Peter 3:15 model as described in chapter 2 of this book. You might even want to point out *sura* 16:125 of the *Qur'an,* which is similar to 1 Peter 3:15. This *sura* exhorts Muslims to "invite all to the way of thy Lord with wisdom and beautiful preaching, and argue with them in ways that are best and most gracious."

• Most Muslims in America are educated and well informed. Be prepared to present the gospel intellectually.

- Many Muslims feel vulnerable, and since most of them have come from collectivist societies, they yearn for a community to join. Start by inviting your Muslim friend to a nonthreatening church activity—a picnic, a concert, Easter and Christmas plays, and so on. Inviting a Muslim over for a meal is another great honor you can bestow. The idea here is to build a friendship over time. Muslims will be more open to hear what you have to say once you have built a relationship with them.
- The Muslim religion prohibits the consumption of pork or alcohol.
- Don't treat the Bible or the *Qur'an* disrespectfully. Don't throw it around, lay it on the ground, or let it touch your feet. Muslims also consider writing in the Bible or *Qur'an* disrespectful, so avoid doing so in front of a Muslim.
- Avoid conversations about *jihad* and terrorism. Most American Muslims are traditionalists and have strong conservative values on issues such as abortion and family.
- Avoid the temptation to label Allah as an evil god. Think of it this way: If a Muslim were to assert that Jesus is an evil god and that Allah is the only true savior, how open would you be to hearing anything about Islam after that point? Many well-meaning but zealous Christians have turned off their Muslim friends with this simple yet devastating error.
- Respect, respect, respect! Never make fun of Allah, Muhammad, or any Muslim religious symbols. Doing so would be a sure way to turn off your listener.
- Muslims who have become Christians will often say that the most convincing argument for following Christ was the love and steadfast friendship Christians showed them.
- If your Muslim friend is of European descent, chances are he or she embraced Islam as a result of feeling marginalized by society and the church. Concentrate on showing your friend that your church is a place where people genuinely care about one another.
- Give a copy of a paraphrased New Testament to your Muslim friend and encourage him or her to read the Gospels.
- Be sensitive to your Muslim friend or coworker during the month of

Ramadan, when Muslims fast from dawn to dusk for an entire month. This is actually a good opportunity to build bridges. Invite your Muslim friend and his or her family for dinner or take dinner to his or her house (after dusk, of course). Take care to observe Islamic dietary rules; if in doubt, ask your Muslim friend.

- It is important to remember that accepting Christ could have serious consequences for most Muslims. Muslims who convert may be disowned by their family and friends. Be patient and supportive of your Muslim friend if he or she is struggling spiritually. The road to salvation in Christ is a tough one for most Muslims and has a costly price tag. Yet we must encourage them to see the priceless gift that Christ has already provided for them.
- Keep a smile on your face and change the subject as soon as you see a discussion turning into a heated argument. You cannot win someone to Christ by arguing or debating with them. Change the topic, reaffirm your love and friendship, and postpone the spiritual discussion for another time.
- Share your personal testimony. This can be a powerful tool in the hands of the Holy Spirit. Prepare your thoughts in advance and keep your story short and simple. Don't use words or phrases such as *convicted*, *filled with the Spirit*, and *born again*, which are meaningless to Muslims.
- Don't forget Who does the saving.

### African American Muslims

According to scholars, Islam first came to America through African slaves. It gained more prominence in the twentieth century, especially since the 1960s. About 42 percent of all Muslims in America are African Americans. Although many believe that African Americans turned to Islam as a protest against whites, this cannot be held as a valid argument under today's social circumstances.

Many Americans connect African American Muslims with the Nation of Islam. The Nation of Islam was started by Wallace Ford but gained prominence under the leadership of Elijah Muhammad, who preached separatism. After his death in 1975 his son directed followers to traditional Islam. Louis Farrakhan formed a new "Nation of Islam" and continues to teach separatism. However, even though Louis Farrakhan can attract large crowds, only a tiny fraction of African American Muslims (less than fifty thousand) belong to the Nation of Islam. When you interact with and witness to African American Muslims, follow the same guidelines given above.

## ARAB AMERICANS

There is a misconception among Americans that most, if not all, Arab Americans are Muslims. If you have that stereotypical response, you would be wrong 77 percent of the time! Only 23 percent of Arab Americans are Muslims. About 54 percent are Christians, and another 23 percent follow orthodox religions.

Some estimates say there are about three million Arab Americans in the United States, most of whom were born here. They are well integrated into American society and can be found in all fifty states, although the largest concentrations of Arab Americans are in California, Michigan, and New York.

Many Arab Americans feel vulnerable after the 2001 attacks on the United States. This time of vulnerability is actually a wonderful opportunity for Christians across the nation to reach out to Arab Americans in love, acceptance, and friendship. It is okay to ask about their culture and heritage. Since most are native-born Americans, standard greeting etiquette applies (although among new immigrants, men should wait for women to initiate shaking hands).

## ORGANIZATIONS

American Muslim Council
1212 New York Avenue, NW #400
Washington, DC 20005
www.amconline.org

Council on American-Islamic Relations
453 New Jersey, SE
Washington, DC 20003-4034
www.cair-net.org

Institute of Islamic Information and Education
P.O. Box 41129
Chicago, IL 60641-0129
www.iiie.net

Islamic Society of North America
P.O. Box 38
Plainfield, IN 46168
www.isna.net

Muslim Peace Fellowship
P.O. Box 271
Nyack, NY 10960
www.mpfweb.org

Muslim Public Affairs Council
994 National Press Building
529 14th Street, NW
Washington, DC 20045
www.mpac.org

Muslim World League
P.O. Box 537
Makkah al-Mukarramah
Saudi Arabia

## FURTHER READING

Ahmed, Akbar S. *Islam Today: A Very Short Introduction.* London: I. B. Taurus and Co., 1999.

Barakat, Halim. *The Arab World: Society, Culture, and State.* Berkeley and Los Angeles: University of California Press, 1993.

Denny, Frederick M. *An Introduction to Islam.* New York: Macmillan, 1994.

Eastman, Roger, ed. *The Ways of Religion.* 3d ed. New York: Oxford University Press, 1999.

Esposito, John L. *Islam: The Straight Path.* 3d ed. New York: Oxford University Press, 1988.

Haneef, Suzanne. *What Everyone Should Know About Islam and Muslims.* 14th ed. Chicago: Library of Islam, 1996.

Lippman, Thomas W. *Understanding Islam: An Introduction to the Muslim World.* 2d rev. ed. New York: Penguin Putnam, Meridian, 1995.

Martinson, Paul Varo, ed. *Islam: An Introduction for Christians.* Trans. Stefanie Ormsby Cox. Minneapolis: Augsburg Fortress, 1994.

McDowell, Josh. *Evidence That Demands a Verdict.* 2 vols. Nashville: Nelson, 1993.

Renard, John. *Responses to 101 Questions on Islam.* New York: Paulist Press, 1998.

Shah, Idries. *The Way of the Sufi.* New York: Penguin Putnam, 1991.

Strobel, Lee. *The Case for Christ.* Grand Rapids: Zondervan, 1998.

Zepp, Ira G., Jr. *A Muslim Primer.* 2d ed. Fayetteville, Ark.: University of Arkansas Press, 2000.

# 16

# Jews

## QUICK FACTS

- Jews believe in one God: the God of the Old Testament.
- Jews believe God has a special relationship with the Jewish people.
- Jews do not believe in the New Testament. Many are familiar with the C. S. Lewis premise of Jesus' being either a liar, a lunatic, or Lord. Many Jews believe that the writers of the New Testament fabricated much of what was written and that the gospel story never really happened as reported.
- The kosher laws (or dietary rules) can be found in the book of Leviticus in the Bible and also in the Jewish Torah.
- Most Jews live in the United States, Israel, Canada, Russia, Poland, Australia, parts of Asia, Europe, and South America. About 44 percent of all Jews live in America. The United States has more Jews than any other country (5.6 to 6.1 million). Another 5 million live in Israel.

## ORIGIN

What the Jewish people consider to be their history can be found in the Old Testament. Abraham is generally considered to be the first Jew. The Jewish people believe they descended from Abraham's son, Isaac. Isaac's son Jacob (or Israel) had twelve sons, who went on to become the twelve tribes of Israel. Moses led the Israelites out of Egyptian bondage, after which time, Saul, David, and Solomon each ruled Israel. After the rule of Solomon, the nation of Israel split into the northern kingdom (Israel), which was made up of ten tribes, and the southern kingdom (Judah), which was made up of two tribes. Both kingdoms were invaded, and the Jewish people were scattered all over the world. In 1948, with the recommendation of the United Nations, the nation of Israel was formed, and Jewish people from all over the world started returning to their homeland.

## SACRED TEXTS

The Jewish scriptures contain the following sections (much of this makes up the Old Testament, although Jews don't refer to it by that name):

1. *Torah.* The *Torah* (which literally means "teaching") is made up of the Pentateuch, or the first five books of the Bible. Jews look to the Torah to learn about their history as a people and also for guidelines for daily living. The Torah is kept inside a replica of the ark of the covenant in each synagogue. Both the contents and the physical book of the Torah are considered sacred by Jews. The Torah is read aloud in the synagogues.

2. *Neviim.* Made up of Joshua, Judges, 1 and 2 Samuel, 1 and 2 Kings, Isaiah, Jeremiah, Ezekiel, and the Minor Prophets. Short selections are read at synagogues, often supplementing the Torah readings.

3. *Ketuvim.* Also known as the Writings, this section contains the books of Psalms, Proverbs, Job, Song of Songs, Ruth, Lamentations, Ecclesiastes, Esther, Daniel, Ezra, Nehemiah, and 1 and 2 Chronicles. Jews are encouraged to use the book of Psalms in their devotions.

Another sacred text in addition to the Jewish scriptures is the *Talmud.* The word *talmud* means "to study." The Talmud fills many volumes and comprises commentaries about Jewish law as well as parables and proverbs. Considered to be the primary source for interpreting Jewish law, it explains how to apply the rules mentioned in the Torah to daily living.

## BELIEFS AND PRACTICES

Jews vary widely in how they practice their religion. Some flout basic dietary rules while others strictly observe the Sabbath.

## The Three Essentials

The three essentials of the Jewish faith include: (1) learning, (2) worship of God, and (3) good works.

For centuries Jews required that all children, whether rich or poor, be educated. By inculcating good qualities, one worships God. These qualities include

### The Jewish Scriptures

1. *Torah*
   - Genesis
   - Exodus
   - Leviticus
   - Numbers
   - Deuteronomy

2. *Neviim*
   - Joshua
   - Judges
   - 1 and 2 Samuel
   - 1 and 2 Kings
   - Isaiah
   - Jeremiah
   - Ezekiel
   - The Twelve Prophets (Hosea, Joel, Amos, Obadiah, Jonah, Micah, Nahum, Habakkuk, Zephaniah, Haggai, Zechariah, and Malachi)

3. *Ketuvim*
   - Psalms
   - Proverbs
   - Job
   - Song of Songs
   - Ruth
   - Lamentations
   - Ecclesiastes
   - Esther
   - Daniel
   - Ezra
   - Nehemiah
   - 1 and 2 Chronicles

kindness, mercy, and compassion. Good works should come from the heart. One should provide for one's needy fellowmen.

## Other Beliefs

Many Jews believe that God is a Spirit being who does not take on human form. They also believe that each person is responsible for his or her own actions and that whether one is a faithful Jew is what will be judged at the end of one's life. Most Jews, at least in practice, do not accept the concept of original sin. God will not punish someone for the sins of Adam and Eve. Rather, we will all be judged on whether we have lived according to God's given laws. If someone does commit sin, he or she can turn to God in repentance for forgiveness. Therefore, a Savior (the way Christians understand it) is not really needed. Many Jews do not believe in the coming of the Messiah.

## Four Types of Judaism

To better understand what Jews believe, take a look at the four major followings within Judaism:

1.  *Orthodox Judaism.* Orthodox Jews believe in the absolute authority of the Torah and follow strict customs and traditions pertaining to dress, the Sabbath, dietary laws, segregation of the sexes in synagogues, and so on.
2.  *Reform Judaism.* Reform Jews are more liberal in their interpretation of the Torah. They place less emphasis on rituals and customs; for example, men and women can sit together, women can be rabbis, and services may be held on Sunday rather than Saturday. They stress learning and using the Torah as an instructional guide. They want to keep Judaism relevant to modern society by constantly reforming it. The Reform movement became popular among Jews in the United States. Reform Jews are sometimes referred to as liberal Jews.
3.  *Conservative Judaism.* Conservative Jews try to find middle ground between Orthodox and Reform Judaism. They retain some traditions and customs but also emphasize interpreting the Torah in light of

modern circumstances. They try to blend tradition with the changing times.

4. *Reconstructionist Judaism.* The most recent and radical of all Jews, Reconstructionists value Judaism as a cultural identity rather than a religious one. Some may not even regard the Torah as divinely inspired or as the ultimate truth.

## The Specifics

1. *God.* God, the same God of the Old Testament, is omnipotent and omniscient.
2. *Creation.* God created the universe and everything in it. Jews embrace the same creation story as Christians do.
3. *Sin.* Jews do not believe in original sin. Sin is breaking God's laws. We disobey God when we break His laws. But we can repent and be granted forgiveness because God is a God of mercy.
4. *Salvation.* After one's death God will judge a person based on his or her works. Heaven is the reward for those who have been faithful. Hell is reserved for those who are evil and unfaithful to God.

### *American Cities with the Largest Jewish Population*

1. New York
2. Los Angeles
3. Miami
4. Philadelphia
5. Chicago
6. Boston

*Source:* Nicholas De Lange, *An Introduction to Judaism* (New York: Cambridge University Press, 2000).

## How to Witness to a Jew

Before you continue, make sure you have read chapter 13 for general guidelines. Jews in America may be of European, Asian, or even African descent. So look up country-specific information in part 2 so that you are aware of additional culture-specific customs and worldviews. Keep in mind that this is not an exhaustive treatment of the subject, but a quick snapshot view.

### The God/Man Separation Issue

One of the best and simplest ways to communicate the gospel is through the gulf diagram that shows the gulf of sin separating God and man. In Christianity, we believe that, by His death on the cross, Jesus Christ bridged the gulf of sin that separates us from God, making it possible for us to know God and have a relationship with Him. (See the gulf diagram on page 189.)

In view of the gulf diagram, let's consider what Judaism says:

|  | **God** | **Chasm** | **Bridge** | **Salvation** |
|---|---|---|---|---|
| **Christianity** | Personal, knowable | Sin | Christ | Eternity with God in heaven |
| **Judaism** | Personal, knowable | Sinful actions | Repentance, good works | Intimacy with God in heaven |

Jews believe in most of the Old Testament, so begin your conversation with points of agreement, including the God of the Old Testament, the creation of the universe, Abraham, Moses, the Ten Commandments, and so on. Many Jews consider the *King James* translation the most accurate, so use this version if you can. Keep in mind that Jews follow only the Old Testament portion of it.

The greatest difficulty for a Jew is accepting Christ as Savior. It will help you to do a careful study of the Old Testament prophecies concerning the Messiah and how those prophecies were fulfilled in the life of Jesus Christ. Read Josh McDowell's *Evidence That Demands a Verdict* or Lee Strobel's *The Case for Christ*. To get you started, here are several Old Testament prophecies and how Jesus Christ fulfilled them:

- Messiah will be born in Bethlehem (Micah 5:2; fulfilled in Matthew 2:1-6).
- Messiah will be born of a virgin (Isaiah 7:14; fulfilled in Matthew 1:18-25).
- Messiah will be rejected by His own people (Isaiah 53:1-3; fulfilled in John 12:37-38).

- Messiah will be betrayed by one of His followers (Psalm 41:9; fulfilled in Matthew 26:47-50).
- Messiah will be tried and condemned (Isaiah 53:8; fulfilled in Luke 23:1-25).
- Messiah will be struck and spat upon (Isaiah 50:6; fulfilled in Matthew 26:67).
- Messiah will be given vinegar (Psalm 69:21; fulfilled in John 19:28-30).
- Messiah's bones will not be broken (Exodus 12:46 and Psalm 34:20; fulfilled in John 19:31-36).
- Messiah will be raised from the dead (Psalm 16:10; fulfilled in Matthew 28:1-10; see also Acts 2:22-32).*

*Keep in Mind...*

Here are some specific guidelines to keep in mind when sharing the gospel with Jews:

- Follow the 1 Peter 3:15 model as described in chapter 2 of this book.
- If meeting a Jew over a meal, be mindful of the strict dietary rules most Jews in this country follow. Foods that are allowed are known as *kosher*. Certain kinds of fish, pork, and some portions of meat are prohibited. Even food that is allowed must be prepared a certain way. If in doubt, ask your Jewish friend ahead of time.
- You can also make a connection with Jewish friends during their many festivals. Christians may recognize the biblical reasons behind many of the Jewish festivals. Major holidays are:

  *Rosh Hashanah*—the Jewish New Year, announced by blowing a ram's horn *(shofar)*.

  *Hanukkah*—Festival of Lights celebrating the recapture of the temple in Jerusalem in 164 B.C. and the miracle of the one-day supply of oil that lasted for eight days.

---

* While I've provided single-fulfillment references from the New Testament, there may be fulfillment passages in other books of the New Testament as well. Use the concordance feature of your Bible to cross-reference these passages.

*Yom Kippur*—ten days after Rosh Hashanah. It is considered a holy day on which Jews make atonement for their sins.

*Pesach*—remembering the freedom from Egyptian bondage.

*Purim*—commemorating Esther and the freedom of the Jewish people.

*Shavuot*—celebrating the receiving of the Ten Commandments.

- Mention the fact that Jesus was a Jew and that many of the first Christians were Jews as well.
- Be very respectful of the Torah and the Bible, both their contents and the books themselves.
- If there is someone in your church who used to be a Jew, connect him or her with your Jewish friend.
- Jews who have become Christians will often say that the most convincing argument for following Christ was the consistent love and friendship that Christians showed them.
- Keep a smile on your face and change the subject if you see the discussion turning into an argument. We rarely win people to Christ by arguing or debating with them. Change the topic, reaffirm your love and friendship, and postpone the spiritual discussion for another time.
- Your personal testimony can be a powerful tool in the hands of the Holy Spirit. Prepare your story in advance and keep it short and simple. Don't use buzz words such as *convicted* and *born again*.
- Don't forget Who does the saving.

## ORGANIZATIONS

American Jewish Committee
P.O. Box 705
New York, NY 10150
www.ajc.org


Union of American Hebrew Congregations
633 Third Avenue
New York, NY 10017
www.uahc.org

## FURTHER READING

De Lange, Nicholas. *An Introduction to Judaism.* New York: Cambridge University Press, 2000.

Donin, Hayim Halevy. *To Be a Jew.* New York: Basic Books, 2001.

Hertzberg, Arthur. *The Jews in America.* New York: Columbia University Press, 1997.

———, and Aron Hirt-Manheimer. *Jews: The Essence and Character of a People.* San Francisco: HarperSanFrancisco, 1998.

Kertzer, Rabbi Morris N. *What Is a Jew?* New York: Simon and Schuster, 1997.

McDowell, Josh. *Evidence That Demands a Verdict.* 2 vols. Nashville: Nelson, 1993.

Strobel, Lee. *The Case for Christ.* Grand Rapids: Zondervan, 1998.

# 17

# Buddhists

## Quick Facts

- There are more than 350 million Buddhists in the world. About 5 million of them are in the United States, and this number is growing.
- There are hundreds of different sects and subsects within Buddhism.
- A Buddhist should not be disturbed when meditating.
- Although Buddha did not claim to be God, many Buddhists believe he was God.
- Tibetan Buddhism has entered mainstream America through the Free Tibet movement, the Dalai Lama, and also through Hollywood personalities such as Richard Gere and Steven Seagal.
- There are hundreds of Buddhist "churches" or centers in the United States.
- Most Buddhists live in Cambodia, China, Japan, Korea, Laos, Mongolia, Myanmar, Sri Lanka, Thailand, Tibet, and Vietnam. Buddhists can be found all over the world. Ironically, there are very few Buddhists in India, the birthplace of Buddhism.

## Origin

Buddhism was founded in India by Siddhartha Gautama more than twenty-five hundred years ago. He was the son of a king who shielded him from suffering. During some of his outings, the young prince saw an old man, a sick man, a corpse, and a holy man. This greatly disturbed him. Siddhartha gave up his inheritance, took on the robes of a poor man, and traveled extensively to find the truth.

One day, while he was meditating under a tree, he was assailed by all kinds of temptations. Buddhists believe these were brought upon him by the Evil One who did not want him to attain enlightenment. Siddhartha successfully warded off these temptations. Suddenly he received knowledge about his previous lives and the truth behind the cycle of birth and rebirth. He solved the mystery of human suffering.

On that day Prince Siddhartha became Buddha, the "Enlightened One." Over the next four and half decades, Buddha traveled and preached his message of salvation. In the third century B.C., Ashoka, the king of most of the (present-day) Indian subcontinent, converted to Buddhism and sent missionaries overseas to preach Buddha's message. Buddhism quickly spread all over Asia.

## SACRED TEXTS

For a long time, Buddha's teachings were passed on orally. When his teachings were finally collected, the *sutras* (Buddhist teachings) and the *sastras* (commentaries) were combined to make up volumes of Buddhist holy text.

---

### What Does It Mean?

*Lama*—a spiritual teacher under Tibetan Buddhism

*Roshi*—a Zen master

*Sangha*—the basic institution where traditions are passed on. Members are exhorted to live in peace with everyone else.

*Sutras*—Buddhist teachings

---

## BELIEFS AND PRACTICES

It is important to note that since Buddhism has hundreds of sects and subsects, beliefs and practices vary from sect to sect.

Overall, Buddhism teaches how to escape suffering and attain salvation.

Salvation *(Nirvana)* is a state of perfect peace and freedom from suffering. Buddha never really explained what this actually means or what Nirvana will really be like, but many of his followers have. Some say Nirvana is an actual place; others say it is a state of being. Although Buddha accepted the Hindu teaching that salvation is freedom from birth and rebirth, he rejected the Hindu idea that salvation also ensures that a person becomes one with God. Buddha did not believe in God.

### The Four Noble Truths

There are several rules of conduct in Buddhism. They begin with the Four Noble Truths:

1. There is suffering in this world (there are more tears than water in the oceans).
2. Suffering is the outcome of desires (or sensual pleasures).
3. Suffering can be overcome by eliminating desires.
4. Freedom from desires can be attained through meditation and by practicing the Eightfold Path.

### The Eightfold Path

Practicing the Eightfold Path enables one to be free of desires. The Eightfold Path consists of the following characteristics:

1. *Right View*—a proper understanding of the Four Noble Truths
2. *Right Thought*—avoiding harm to others and all forms of life
3. *Right Speech*—avoiding unkind words, gossip, and lies
4. *Right Action*—good deeds and being morally right
5. *Right Livelihood*—employment that doesn't cause harm to others in any way
6. *Right Effort*—focusing time and efforts on good thoughts and productive work
7. *Right Mindfulness*—spending time in self-introspection, being compassionate, etc.
8. *Right Contemplation*—spending time in meditation, thereby disciplining the mind

## Other Teachings

Buddhists are taught to be a part of the *Sangha,* the fellowship of other Buddhists. They are also taught to avoid hatred, destruction of life, telling lies, any kind of impurity, stealing, intoxicants, and sexual misconduct. The more devout Buddhists may avoid dancing, singing, jewelry, silver, gold, and perfume. They may also not eat at certain times of the day. On the day of the full moon, Buddhists usually visit their temples or spend time studying and meditating on Buddhist scriptures.

## The Major Sects

Of the hundreds of sects and subsects in Buddhism, some of the major ones include:

1. *Theravada. Theravada* means "way of the elders." In Buddhism there is a lot of respect for monks and nuns. This sect teaches that there are no gods and that Buddha was human. Theravada is practiced in Bangladesh, Cambodia, Laos, Myanmar, Sri Lanka, and Thailand.
2. *Mahayana.* This sect believes that Buddha was a god and refers to him as "The Buddha," since there have been and will be other Buddhas. Mahayana is practiced in China, Japan, Korea, Mongolia, and Tibet. It has numerous sects and subsects.
3. *Zen.* Zen Buddhism is actually a subsect within Mahayana Buddhism, but it has found increasing popularity in the West. Zen Buddhism emphasizes meditation as the only way to salvation. Zen Buddhists do not follow any religious rituals.
4. *Vajrayana.* Vajrayana Buddhists practice rituals and believe they can achieve salvation by following Buddhist teachings. This form of Buddhism is practiced mainly in China, India, Japan, and Tibet. One branch of Vajrayana Buddhism is Tibetan Buddhism, which follows the Dalai Lama as its spiritual leader and considers him a reincarnation of all his predecessors.

## THE SPECIFICS

1. *God.* Buddha did not claim to be God, but some of his followers deify him.

2. *Creation.* Since there is no God, there was no creation.

3. *Sin.* The suffering in this world is the result of desires, not sin.

4. *Salvation.* Salvation can be achieved by following Buddhist teachings as outlined above. It transports a Buddhist to a state of perfect peace and the absence of suffering.

## How to Witness to a Buddhist

Before you continue, make sure you have read chapter 13 for general guidelines. Also, look up country-specific information in part 2 so that you are aware of additional culture-specific customs and worldviews. Keep in mind that this is not an exhaustive treatment of the subject, but a quick snapshot view.

### The God/Man Separation Issue

One of the best and simplest ways to communicate the gospel is through the gulf diagram that shows the gulf of sin separating God and man. In Christianity, we believe that, by His death on the cross, Jesus Christ bridged the gulf of sin that separates us from God, making it possible for us to know God and have a relationship with Him. (See the gulf diagram on page 189.)

With that simple diagram in mind, let's consider what Buddhism says:

|  | God | Chasm | Bridge | Salvation |
|---|---|---|---|---|
| Christianity | Personal, knowable | Sin | Christ | Eternity with God in heaven |
| Buddhism | Some believe there is no God, while others believe Buddha was a god. Buddha himself did not claim to be a god. | Suffering | Cessation of desires by following Buddhist teachings | A perfect state of peace and the absence of suffering |

Once you study this chart, you will be able to provide a credible case as to why following Christ makes sense. For example, can desire ever be totally eliminated from our earthly lives? After all, we do have legitimate needs such as food, clothing, and shelter. Can anyone be perfect or good enough to bridge the gap between God and man? Even if, through some herculean effort, a person managed for a short span of time to completely forsake all desires, can anyone sustain this without ever stumbling for the rest of life? Is this way of living practical? What happens when we die? What does Nirvana really mean? What does a state of perfect peace mean? Where does it exist?

Some other questions to pose:

1. *God.* If there is no God, how do you explain order and method in the universe? (If your Buddhist friend says Buddha was a god, then point out that Buddha himself never claimed to be a god.)

2. *Creation.* How did we get here? How did the universe get its present form? If the universe had no beginning (as Buddhists believe), how is it that scientists have proven that the universe is slowing down? How did the different forms of life on earth get here?

3. *Sin.* How do you explain man's sinful nature? (Because of their belief that there was no original sin and that human beings can work out their own salvation through good works, this one is especially tough for many Buddhists to explain.) If we are capable of working out our own salvation and if we don't believe in original sin, then why is there evil in this world? Why is there sin? Why do men and women do things that are clearly wrong? Why are men and women different from the rest of creation?

## Keep in Mind…

Here are some specific guidelines to keep in mind when sharing with Buddhists:

- Follow the 1 Peter 3:15 model as described in chapter 2 of this book.
- Find out what sect your Buddhist friend belongs to and learn as much as possible about that sect's specific beliefs about God, creation, sin, and salvation. I have provided a list of helpful additional resources at the end of this chapter.
- Search for common ground such as the fact that there is suffering in this world, that Western society is materialistic, and that people do search for meaning in life.

- Never take your Buddhist friend to a hamburger place. Most Buddhists are vegetarians and would be greatly insulted to be invited to a restaurant where beef is served. By the same token, most Buddhists avoid leather products.
- Do not label Buddha as an evil god, evil spirit, or a demon. Think of it this way: If a Buddhist were to tell you that Jesus is an evil god and that Buddha is the only true Savior, how open would you be to hearing anything about Buddhism? Many well-meaning but zealous Christians have turned off their Buddhist friends by this simple yet devastating error.
- Christians who were once Buddhists will often say that the most convincing argument for following Christ was the love and friendship Christians showed them.
- Broach the topic of the cycle of birth and rebirth and salvation. Listen first. Then use the gulf diagram (page 189) to explain that Christ provides an answer for how salvation can be achieved. It is difficult for a Buddhist to accept that salvation can be achieved without any work on the individual's part. Ask, "Can anyone be perfect or good enough to achieve salvation by his or her own means?"
- Keep a smile on your face. If you see the discussion turning into a heated argument, stop. We rarely win people to Christ by arguing or debating with them. Change the topic, reaffirm your love and friendship, and postpone the spiritual discussion for another time.
- Share your personal testimony. This can be a powerful tool in the hands of the Holy Spirit. Prepare your story in advance and keep it short and simple. Don't use words or phrases such as *convicted, filled with the Spirit,* or *born again,* which are meaningless to a Buddhist.
- Don't forget Who does the saving.

## ORGANIZATIONS
Buddhist Churches of America
1710 Octavia Street
San Francisco, CA 94109

Buddhist Society for Compassionate Wisdom
1710 W. Cornelia Avenue
Chicago, IL 60657
www.zenbuddhisttemple.org

Maple Buddhist Society
9089 Richmond
Brossard, QC J4X 2S1
Canada

Society for Buddhist-Christian Studies
St. Edwards University
3906 Balcone Woods Drive
Austin, TX 78759
www.cssr.org

*Tricycle: The Buddhist Review*
92 Vandam Street
New York, NY 10013
www.tricycle.com
Provides a listing of all Zen Centers in the United States

A list of Buddhist churches in America may be found at www.fogbank.com/bca.

## FURTHER READING

Armstrong, Karen. *Buddha.* New York: Penguin Putnam, Viking, 2001.

Carus, Paul, comp. *The Teachings of Buddha.* Rev. ed. New York: St. Martin's Press, 1998.

Carrithers, Michael. *The Buddha: A Very Short Introduction.* New York: Oxford University Press, 2001.

Erricker, Clive, *Teach Yourself Buddhism.* New York: McGraw-Hill, Contemporary Books, 1995.

Kornfield, Jack, and Gil Fronsdal, eds. *Teachings of the Buddha*. Boston: Shambhala Publications, 1996.

McDowell, Josh. *Evidence That Demands a Verdict*. 2 vols. Nashville: Nelson, 1993.

Scheck, Frank Rainer, and Manfred Görgens. *Buddhism*. New York: Barron's, 1999.

Stokes, Gillian. *Buddha: A Beginner's Guide*. London: Hodder and Stoughton, 2000.

Strobel, Lee. *The Case for Christ*. Grand Rapids: Zondervan, 1998.

# 18

# Other Religions

Before you attempt to witness to people who follow these religions, review the 1 Peter 3:15 model in chapter 2. Also see chapter 13 for general guidelines for interacting with people of other religions.

## CONFUCIANISM

This religion was founded by Confucius (551–479 B.C.), who traveled all across China with his teachings on individual morality and the proper use of political power. Confucianism is more a set of ethics to live by than a religion. Confucius never wanted to start a religion, although his followers deified him. Some rituals have been woven in over the years and take place during different phases in one's life (birth, maturity, marriage, and death).

Confucius emphasized the development of character and moral values, including politeness, etiquette, respect for the elderly, righteous living, moderation, loyalty to the state, and the highest all of virtues: consideration toward others.

There are no accurate figures as to the number of people who practice Confucianism, as many may also practice other religions. Estimates put the number between six and three hundred million. Confucianism is principally practiced in China, Japan, Korea, and certain Southeast Asian countries. In the United States it is also largely practiced among people who trace their heritage to these countries.

## How to Witness to a Confucian: The God/Man Separation Issue

Since Confucius did not attach much importance to God (or gods, as he thought it), it is difficult to pinpoint specifics in the God/Man Separation dilemma. Still, using the gulf diagram presented earlier (page 189), Confucianism and Christianity relate as follows:

|              | God                                                                                              | Chasm          | Bridge                                              | Salvation                                                                                                                    |
|--------------|--------------------------------------------------------------------------------------------------|----------------|-----------------------------------------------------|------------------------------------------------------------------------------------------------------------------------------|
| Christianity | Personal, knowable                                                                               | Sin            | Christ                                              | Eternity with God in heaven                                                                                                  |
| Confucianism | Impersonal, more or less unattached to humankind (many revere Confucius as a god)                | Wrongful deeds | Follow the many virtues taught by Confucius         | Life after death is not addressed, so salvation becomes an earthly goal of leading a good life (dependent upon oneself)      |

Once you study this chart, you will be able to provide a credible case as to why following Christ makes sense. For example, how can one have a relationship with an impersonal god? How did humans get here? How did Creation take place? How do you explain order and method in the universe? Is this life all there is, or is there life after death? If there is life after death, how can one prepare for it? Since many Confucianists believe in gods, talk about the roles of these gods. What do they do in contrast to the God of the Bible? Can anyone be perfect or good enough to bridge the gap between humans and God? If a person can attain a perfect life by him- or herself, why are there gods? How can one have a relationship with a God who is unknowable and impersonal? Why is there evil in the world?

Keep in mind that many Confucianists see their religion as part of their culture. They may also view Christianity as a Western religion. Talk about Christianity's origin: It began in the Middle East, not in America or Europe.

Share your personal testimony, and don't forget Who does the saving.

## Further Reading

Cleary, Thomas. *The Essential Confucius.* San Francisco: HarperSanFrancisco, 1992.

Leys, Simon. *The Analects of Confucius.* New York: W. W. Norton and Company, 1997.

## JAINISM

Mahavira, who grew up in a royal family in India around the sixth century B.C., is considered to be the founder of Jainism. He is also called the "Great Hero." When he was about thirty years old, Mahavira gave up all earthly possessions and devoted himself to meditation and reflection. During this time he subjected himself to severe physical hardships. Jains believe Mahavira achieved Nirvana (salvation). They also believe he was the last of the twenty-four *Tirthankaras* (great saints).

Jainism started as a reform movement within Hindu India. Jainism teaches that there is no God or Supreme Being; salvation is dependent upon one's own self and works. Salvation comes from being released from the cycle of birth and rebirth; as such, Jains become *Jinas* (victors) just as Mahavira did. No one created the universe; it is eternal, and all living things—even plants—have a soul. Thus, if you are a bad person in this life, you could be born again as a lower life-form or even as a plant. There are several "levels" of heaven and hell, and based upon a person's works—good or bad—he or she may end up at the highest level of heaven or the lowest level of hell.

Jains are known for their sanctity toward any living thing. Jain religion strictly prohibits any kind of killing—even the killing of an insect. Jains are strict vegetarians. Yet even vegetables have life, and just by eating vegetables they are, in fact, killing a life-form. For this reason, Jains confess their sins daily. They also do not consume alcohol or tobacco.

The Jain scriptures were put together hundreds of years after Mahavira's death. They are called the *Agamas* (precepts). Liberation from the cycle of birth and rebirth can be achieved by following three principles: (1) *Right Conviction* (belief in Jain teachings and scriptures); (2) *Right Knowledge* (understanding Jain teachings); and (3) *Right Conduct*.

Right Conduct can be achieved by adhering to the following five principles:

1. practicing nonviolence
2. practicing truthfulness
3. practicing honesty
4. not becoming attached to possessions
5. living a chaste life

There are about ten million Jains in the world, and their number, though small, is increasing in the United States.

### How to Witness to a Jain: The God/Man Separation Issue

In recent years, several Jain organizations have sprung up in the United States. One of the ways you can tell whether a person is a Jain is by looking at last names. Most Jains have Jain or Jaini as their last name.

Jainism denies the existence of God. Placed next to the gulf diagram presented earlier (page 189), Jainism and Christianity stack up as follows:

|  | **God** | **Chasm** | **Bridge** | **Salvation** |
|---|---|---|---|---|
| **Christianity** | Personal, knowable | Sin | Christ | Eternity with God in heaven |
| **Jainism** | There is no God | Wrong deeds of past and this life | Good deeds in this life | Climbing the levels of heaven to achieve Nirvana (salvation) |

Once you study this chart, you will be able to present a credible case as to why following Christ makes sense. For example, if there is no God, how did we get here? How, then, are order and method present in the universe? Can anyone really be perfect or good enough to attain Nirvana? Even if, through some extraordinary herculean effort, someone managed to achieve nothing but good deeds over a short period of time, can anyone sustain this without ever stumbling for the rest of his or her life? How can one practice the principle of nonviolence (*ahimsa*) when one eats vegetables daily? Why is there sin? Why do men and women do things that are clearly wrong? Why are men and women different from the rest of creation? Who created heaven and hell?

Keep in mind that Jains are strict vegetarians. Some may even avoid eating anything that comes from the roots of plants. Do not eat meat, eggs, or fish in front of a Jain. By the same token, most Jains avoid products made from animals, such as leather products. Never make fun of or otherwise denigrate the Jain belief that even vegetables and microorganisms could have been humans in their previous lives.

Broach the topic of the cycle of birth and rebirth and salvation. Listen first, then use the gulf diagram (page 189) to explain that Jesus Christ provides an answer for how salvation can be achieved. It is difficult for a Jain to accept that salvation can be achieved without any work on the individual's part. Ask, "Can anyone be perfect or good enough to achieve salvation by his or her own means?"

Share your personal testimony, and don't forget Who does the saving.

### Organizations
Brahmi Jain Society and Mahavir World Vision, Inc (*Jain Spirit* magazine)
1884 Dorsetshire Road
Columbus, OH 43229
www.jainspirit.org

Jain World
www.jainworld.com (This Web site links to Jain societies all around the world.)

Federations of Jain Associations in North America
P.O. Box 700
Getzville, NY 14068
www.jaina.org

## Shintoism
Shintoism is Japan's indigenous religion, but it doesn't have a founder. Nine out of ten Japanese people visit Shinto shrines. They are often willing to combine Shintoism with Buddhism or Christianity.

An ancient Japanese religion, Shintoism follows the way of the *Kami*, seeing divinity in almost everything. Consequently, Shintoists see all of life as sacred, and nature is to be revered. Shinto mythology also affirms that members of Japanese royalty have descended directly from the sun goddess.

Shintoists believe that the sacred spirits live in nature. Hence, Shintoists frequently worship trees, and it is not uncommon to find large quantities of trees around Shinto shrines. Shintoists believe that humans are basically good, so salvation through a savior is unnecessary. There is no concept of original sin or of sin itself.

Some vital teachings of Shintoism include the importance of family and tradition, the love and worship of nature, rituals, and self-purification. (Shintoists remove their shoes and rinse their mouths and hands before entering a shrine.)

Since the religion is combined with the culture, it is difficult for a Shintoist to consider Christianity.

### *How to Witness to a Shintoist: The God/Man Separation Issue*

Most Shintoists live in Japan. Tens of thousands more can be found in North America, and almost all are of Japanese descent. Review the section in chapter 8 on Japan to learn about Japanese culture before you attempt to witness to a Shintoist.

Shintoists believe in many gods and believe that many of them are manifested in nature. Placed next to the gulf diagram presented earlier (page 189), Shintoism and Christianity stack up as follows:

|  | **God** | **Chasm** | **Bridge** | **Salvation** |
|---|---|---|---|---|
| **Christianity** | Personal, knowable | Sin | Christ | Eternity with God in heaven |
| **Shintoism** | Many gods; many manifested in nature | No chasm; man is good | Bridge not needed as there is no chasm | Vague concepts of heaven and hell (usually not a place of eternal bliss or damnation) |

Once you study this chart, you will be able to provide a credible case as to why following Christ makes sense. For example, if man is basically good, why does he do things that are wrong? Why is there evil in this world? Can anyone be perfect or good enough to attain salvation? Even if, through some extraordinary herculean effort, a person managed to achieve nothing but good deeds over a short period of time, can anyone sustain this without ever stumbling for the rest of life? Why do men and women do things that are clearly wrong (sinful)? Why are men and women different from the rest of creation? What exactly are heaven and hell like? What happens when a person dies?

Since Shintoists emphasize purification and cleanliness, make sure you are well groomed when meeting with a Shintoist friend. Personal cleanliness is very important, especially if you visit a Shintoist's home for a special occasion. You must offer to remove your shoes before entering the house, and you may be required to wash your hands and mouth. Never make fun of or otherwise denigrate the Shintoist belief that the gods reside in trees and rocks.

Share your personal testimony, and don't forget Who does the saving.

*Organizations*
International Shinto Foundation
New York Center
777 United Nations Plaza
Suite WCRP-9A
New York, NY 10017
www.shinto.org

## SIKHISM

Sikhism was founded in northern India by Guru Nanak Dev in the fifteenth century. After Guru Nanak, a total of nine Sikh gurus led the Sikh religion. The last of them was Guru Gobind Singh, who died in 1708. Before he died, he told Sikhs to follow the *Guru Granth Sahib,* the sacred text of Sikhism. Sikhs greatly respect this book, the content as well as the book itself. They must never wear shoes in its presence, point their feet toward it, or turn their backs to it. They must also cover their heads in its presence.

Sikhs believe there is a spirit God who created the universe. Salvation is dependent upon good works, and one must continually repent of his or her bad works. Sikhs believe that humans are inherently good; however, they also believe that sin is the result of selfishness. A tally will be made after our deaths; those whose good works total more than their bad works will achieve salvation. For Sikhs, salvation is similar to the Hindu concept of salvation—becoming one with God and enjoying indescribable bliss. Hell is being caught in the cycle of birth and rebirth. Unlike Hindus, Sikhs do not worship idols or believe in the caste system. All people are equal before God.

Sikhs believe that five things make up selfishness or self-centeredness and cause us to move away from God: greed, lust, pride, anger, and attachment to material things. Sikh virtues include worship, prayer, self-control, compassion, patience, charity, service, dignity of labor, and equality of all human beings.

### How to Witness to a Sikh: The God/Man Separation Issue

There are more than one-half million Sikhs in North America. Male Sikhs are easy to spot, as most of them wear a turban on their heads. Sikh turbans should never be confused with the turban worn by Muslims from some countries; the Sikh turban is triangular in shape and peaks above the forehead. The reason for the turban is that men do not cut their hair. Most Sikh men have the last name *Singh;* most Sikh women have the last name *Kaur.*

Since almost all Sikhs are of Indian origin, review the section in chapter 8 on India before you attempt to witness to a Sikh.

Placed next to the gulf diagram presented earlier (page 189), Sikhism and Christianity stack up as follows:

|  | **God** | **Chasm** | **Bridge** | **Salvation** |
|---|---|---|---|---|
| **Christianity** | Personal, knowable | Sin | Christ | Eternity with God in heaven |
| **Sikhism** | Impersonal, unknowable | Selfishness or self-centeredness drives us away from God | Good works | Becoming one with God |

Once you study this chart, you will be able to provide a credible case as to why following Christ makes sense. For example, if man is basically good, why does he do things that are wrong? Why is there evil in this world? Even if, through some herculean effort, a person managed to achieve a short span of time when he does nothing but good deeds, can anyone sustain this without ever stumbling for the rest of his or her life? Why is there sin? Why do men and women do things that are clearly wrong? Why are men and women different from the rest of creation? What exactly are heaven and hell like? What happens when a person dies? What does becoming one with God mean?

Broach the topic of the cycle of birth and rebirth and salvation. Listen first, then use the gulf diagram (page 189) to explain that Christ provides an answer for how salvation can be achieved. It is difficult for a Sikh to accept that salvation can be achieved without any work on the individual's part. Ask, "Can anyone be perfect or good enough to achieve salvation by his or her own means?"

Also, study the lives of two Sikhs in India who became Christians and made a significant impact among the Sikh community: Sadhu Sundar Singh (one of my heroes of the faith) and Bhakt Singh. Talk about them with your Sikh friend.

Share your personal testimony, and don't forget Who does the saving.

### Organizations

The *Sikhism* home page: www.sikhs.org.

## Epilogue

# Starting a Ministry to Internationals in Your Church

If your church doesn't already have a ministry to internationals, you may want to consider starting one. Talk with your pastoral staff to see how this kind of ministry would fit into the broader vision the Lord has given to your church.

Before you begin, do two very important things: First, pray. Saturate your planning and vision with prayer. Several years ago my wife and I met a lady who worked as a hospital chaplain in Southern California. My wife said to her, "Your role must be tough—visiting sick and dying people every day."

The woman replied, "Oh, no. I see myself simply as God's little gardener. I try to plant His seeds in people, and then it's up to Him to water and tend those seeds."

I have never forgotten that response. That's what we all can be: God's little gardeners. If we just plant the seeds, He will nurture them and make them grow.

The second important thing to do is enlist the help of other people who have a similar burden to reach people of other cultures and religions. Your ministry will be even more effective if you can involve Christians from different cultures who are already part of your church.

Try to figure out which countries or ethnic groups are most prominent in your county and city. You can get this information from the Internet. Check your county government's Web site, your local chamber of commerce, or the U.S. Census Bureau online at www.census.gov. Once you have defined the demographics, find out if there are organizations or associations representing people from any particular country. Approach these associations and ask if you can invite their members to your church. Christmas or Easter programs, concerts, plays, and other special events provide excellent opportunities. Can your church provide refreshments afterward? This would be useful in connecting one-on-one with people.

Many new immigrants struggle with the English language. Could your church provide an English as a Second Language (ESL) class for free or for a nominal fee? Several good texts are available to teach ESL, and a person need not be a professional teacher to lead these classes. Classes can meet once each week for several weeks.

Your church can also organize and host an international dinner. Invite people from different cultural backgrounds to bring their ethnic food for a giant potluck lunch or dinner. This would be a great opportunity for regular members to invite their international friends.

Another effective way to attract people to church is to provide some sort of vocational training workshops. These need not be elaborate. Basic computer skills, for instance, are always in demand. I know of several churches in metro areas that provide U.S. citizenship classes. These attract dozens of internationals, many of whom end up attending the church.

Group sports such as basketball, baseball, or volleyball can provide great opportunities for young people to invite non-Christian and international friends.

Be creative! Think of low-cost services that internationals need. What are some ways the church can meet those needs? What are some friendly, non-threatening ways in which we can bring our international friends to church? How can we create opportunities for them to connect with others within the church?

Whatever you do, saturate your efforts with prayer, asking God to anoint you. He will. The field is ripe for the harvest. Indeed, we can reach the world in our own backyard.

# Bibliography

Acuff, Frank L. *How to Negotiate Anything with Anyone Anywhere Around the World.* New York: American Management Association, AMACOM, 1997.

Anderson, Stevens W., ed. *The Great American Bathroom Book.* Vol. 2. Salt Lake City: Compact Classics, 1993.

"Buddhism in the U.S." *Asia Today,* 18 June 2001. Found at www.asiasource.org/news/at_mp_02.cfm?newsid=54751.

Axtell, Roger E. *Do's and Taboos of Hosting International Visitors.* New York: John Wiley & Sons, 1990.

Barone, Michael, Mike Tharp, Susan Brenna, and David S. Powell. "The Many Faces of America." *U.S. News and World Report,* 19 March 2001. Found at www.usnews.com.

Beech, Hannah. "Don't You Dare List Them as 'Other.'" *U.S. News and World Report,* 8 April 1996. Found at www.usnews.com.

Beversluis, Joel, ed. *Sourcebook of the World's Religions.* 3d ed. Novato, Calif.: New World Library, 2000.

Blank, Jonah. "The Muslim Mainstream." *U.S. News and World Report,* 20 July 1998. Found at www.usnews.com.

Cateora, Philip R., and John L. Graham. *International Marketing.* 11th ed. New York: McGraw-Hill, 2001.

Cohn, D'Vera. "Shifting Portrait of U.S. Hispanics." *Washington Post,* 10 May 2001.

De Lange, Nicholas. *An Introduction to Judaism.* New York: Cambridge University Press, 2000.

De Vries, Mary A. *Internationally Yours.* Boston: Houghton Mifflin, 1994.

Draine, Cathie, and Barbara Hall. *Culture Shock! Indonesia.* Portland, Oreg.: Graphic Arts Center Publishing Company, 1986.

Ellis, Claire. *Culture Shock! Vietnam.* Portland, Oreg.: Graphic Arts Center Publishing Company, 1995.

Engley, Hollis L. "Searching for God in All the New Places." *USA Today,* 27 May 1999. Found at www.usatoday.com/2000/religion/rel001.htm.

Esty, Katharine, Richard Griffin, and Marcie Schorr Hirsch. *Workplace Diversity.* Avon, Mass.: Adams Media Corporation, 1995.

Gaer, Joseph. *How the Great Religions Began.* 1929. Reprint, New York: Dodd, Mead & Company, 1981.

Gleason, Norma, comp. *1,001 Proverbs for Every Occasion.* Secaucus, N.J.: Carol Publishing Group, 1999.

Gonzalez, Juan. *Harvest of Empire: A History of Latinos in America.* New York: Penguin Putnam, Viking, 2000.

Graff, Marie Louise. *Culture Shock! Spain.* Portland, Oreg.: Graphic Arts Center Publishing Company, 1997.

Halter, Marilyn. *Shopping for Identity.* New York: Knopf, Schocken Books, 2000.

Hamilton, Martha M. "Taking Steps to Deal with Diversity in the Workplace." *Washington Post,* 15 March 1993.

Harris, Philip R., and Robert T. Moran. *Managing Cultural Differences.* 4th ed. Houston: Gulf Publishing, 1996.

Harrison, Lawrence E., and Samuel P. Huntington, eds. *Culture Matters: How Values Shape Human Progress.* New York: Basic Books, 2000.

Hur, Sonja Vegdahl, and Ben Seunghwa Hur. *Culture Shock! Korea.* Portland, Oreg.: Graphic Arts Center Publishing Company, 2001.

"Islam Claims Many Followers." *USA Today,* 18 September 2001, 23A.

Joselit, Jenna Weissman. *Immigration and American Religion.* New York: Oxford University Press, 2001.

McDowell, Josh. *Evidence That Demands a Verdict.* 2 vols. Nashville: Nelson, 1993.

Park, Ked, ed. *The World Almanac and Book of Facts, 2002.* New York: World Almanac Books, 2001.

Meacham, Jon. "The New Face of Race." *Newsweek,* 18 September 2000.

Mittmann, Karin, and Zafar Ihsan. *Culture Shock! Pakistan.* Portland, Oreg.: Graphic Arts Center Publishing Company, 1991.

Morrison, Terri, Wayne A. Conaway, and George A. Borden. *Kiss, Bow, or Shake Hands.* Holbrook, Mass.: Adams Media Corporation, 1994.

Reaves, Jessica. "How the Census Colors Our Perception of Racial Issues." *Time,* 13 March 2001. Found at www.time.com/time/nation/article/ 0,8599,102337,00.html.

Roleff, Tamara L., ed. *Immigration: Opposing Viewpoints.* San Diego: Greenhaven Press, 1998.

Sabath, Ann Marie. *International Business Etiquette—Asia and the Pacific Rim.* Franklin Lakes, N.J.: Career Press, 1999.

———. *International Business Etiquette—Europe.* Franklin Lakes, N.J.: Career Press, 1999.

———. *International Business Etiquette—Latin America.* Franklin Lakes, N.J.: Career Press, 2000.

Samovar, Larry, A., Richard E. Porter, and Lisa A. Stefani. *Communication Between Cultures.* 3d ed. Belmont, Calif.: Wadsworth Publishing Company, 1998.

Sheler, Jeffery L., and Michael Betzold. "Muslim in America." *U.S. News and World Report,* 29 October 2001, 50-2.

Sims, Susan M., ed. *CultureGrams: The Nations Around Us.* 2 vols. Lindon, UT: Axiom Press, 2002.

Sinclair, Kevin, and Iris Wong Po-Yee. *Culture Shock! China.* Portland, Oreg.: Graphic Arts Center Publishing Company, 1997.

Strobel, Lee. *The Case for Christ.* Grand Rapids: Zondervan, 1998.

Svensson, Charlotte Rosen. *Culture Shock! Sweden.* Portland, Oreg.: Graphic Arts Center Publishing Company, 1996.

Szumski, Bonnie, ed. *Interracial America: Opposing Viewpoints.* San Diego: Greenhaven Press, 1996.

Van Biema, David. "Backlash: As American As...." *Time,* 1 October 2001, 72-4.

White, Gayle Colquitt. *Believers and Beliefs.* New York: Penguin Putnam, Berkley Books, 1997.

Whoriskey, Peter. "Boom Bolsters Indian Community." *Washington Post,* 27 May 2001.

Williams, Mary E., ed. *Discrimination: Opposing Viewpoints.* San Diego: Greenhaven Press, 1997.

Wilson, Susan L. *Culture Shock! Egypt.* Rev. ed. Portland, Oreg.: Graphic Arts Center Publishing Company, 2001.

Winters, Paul A., ed. *Race Relations: Opposing Viewpoints.* San Diego: Green-haven Press, 1996.


The following Web sites were also very helpful in the preparation of this book:


Central Intelligence Agency, *The CIA World Factbook:* www.odci.gov/cia/ publications/factbook

The U.S. Census Bureau: www.census.gov

# About the Author

RAJENDRA PILLAI was born in Calcutta, India. Having grown up in a Muslim neighborhood in a Hindu nation, Rajendra was acutely conscious of being in the minority as a Christian. Early in life he learned as much as possible about his faith so he could provide an effective Christian response to his many Hindu, Muslim, Buddhist, and Jain friends.

Rajendra has a passion for relating to and reaching people of other cultures. His work experiences have included working with people from forty countries. He has an MBA in Global Economic Development from Eastern University in St. Davids, Pennsylvania.

Rajendra also conducts corporate training in cross-cultural and management issues. He has taught management and cross-cultural relations seminars and courses to organizations, including the National Institutes of Health and the Federal Bureau of Investigation. If you would like to schedule Rajendra for a speaking engagement, or if you would like to know more about his ministry, contact him at:

Reaching the World
P.O. Box 255
Clarksburg, MD 20871-0255

For additional resources and information, please visit his Web site at www.ReachingtheWorld.com or info@ReachingtheWorld.com.

To learn more about WaterBrook Press and view
our catalog of products, log on to our Web site:
**www.waterbrookpress.com**

WATERBROOK
PRESS